RUNNING over FORTY

Other books by Bruce Tulloh

Tulloh On Running
Four Million Footsteps
Naturally Fit
The Teenage Runner
The Olympic Games
The Complete Distance Runner
The Complete Jogger
Bruce Tulloh's Running Log
Running Is Easy

RUNNING over FORTY

Tulloh Books ~ Marlborough

Bruce & Sue Tulloh

Published in 2001 by **Tulloh Books**
The Gatehouse, West Stowell, Marlborough, Wiltshire, SN8 4JU

ISBN 0 95415 210 7

Design by **Tim Barnes** and illustrations by **Katherine Tulloh**: Chicken www.herechickychicky.com

Printed and bound in the UK by **Antony Rowe Ltd**

Contents

Acknowlegdements
Thanks are due to the following for their contributions:
Margaret Auerback, Keith Anderson, Richard Barrington, British Veterans Athletic Federation, Richard Cashmore, John Collins, Frank Copping, Douglas Cowie, Bruce Davidson, Colin Dow, Martin Duff, Bill Foster, Pat Gallagher, Nigel Gates, Jenny Gray, Ralph Henley, Gareth Jones, Steve James, Peter Lee, Terry McCarthy, Mick McGeogh, Jenny Mills, Steve Mottershead, Sharman Patterson, Bob Pape, Martin Rees, Roger Robinson, John Seed, Kevin Shannon, Helen Stokes, Nigel Stuart-Thorn, Jonathan Such, Ted Townsend, Alan Trengove, Ian Vaughan-Arbuckle and all those others who sent in questionnaires.

Photography
Jeremy Hemming: cover, pp. 4, 15, 16, 24, 53, 56, 60, 66, 80, 91, 93, 94, 96, 103, 104, 106, 108, 111, 114, 115, 121, 124, 130, 133
Mark Shearman: pp. xiv, 23, 44, 45, 46, 47, 98, 134, 136, 145, 153
Steven Smythe: pp. 18, 167, 171, 180, 188
Noel Tamini: p. 30 (from *La Saga des Pedestrians)*

**This book is dedicated to all our athletes,
from whom we have learned as much as we have taught**

Introduction

> *"Afoot, light-hearted, I take to the open road,*
> *the long brown path before me leading*
> *wherever I chose."*
>
> **WALT WHITMAN**

Walt Whitman wrote those words in 1870, and no one has been able to improve on them as an expression of the freedom of running.

To you who are reading these words we say: Welcome! Enter the limitless world which the runner enjoys.

Whether you are new to running or have been at it for thirty years, there is always more to learn and more to experience. You will go to places you have never seen before. You will go to some places you will never wish to see again. You will meet all sorts of people and some of them will become your friends. Above all, you will learn more about yourself, and not only in a physical sense. Running can improve you physically and mentally. It can cure depression, improve your appetite and make your legs look better. It can also turn you into a self-obsessed prig – but if that makes you happy...

There is another aspect to running which cannot be found in any other sport, that of taking part in international events alongside the international runners. You cannot kick about on the Wembley turf or join in on the tail of the England innings at Lord's, but you can run in the Great North Run, the London Marathon or the World Veterans Championships and be competing with Olympic champions. Sometimes you can even finish ahead of them!

Personal stuff: Bruce

It may seem egotistical to put this in at the beginning, but I think it will help to explain some of my references later on.

I have been running for well over fifty years and I have been an over-forty for twenty-five years. In my youth I was a good track runner – European champion at 5000m, AAA champion several times, British and European record-holder for ten years, in the days when two mile, three miles and six miles were standard distances. I ran a mile in under four minutes, two miles in eight minutes and 30 seconds, three miles in 13:12 and six miles in 27:23 secs (worth 28:23 for 10k).

I also ran cross-country for twenty years at all levels, from schoolboy to England international. I didn't run many road races, but I did run five miles in twenty-three minutes, ten miles in forty-eight minutes and twenty miles in 101 minutes. In eleven years of serious competition I ran six hundred races, travelled everywhere and met most of the world's leading runners and coaches – men such as Arthur Lydiard, Mihaly Igloi and Percy Cerutty, runners such as Emil Zatopek, Murray Halberg and Gordon Pirie. After I retired from the track I ran from Los Angeles to New York, covering the 3000 miles in sixty-five days and beating the previous record by eight days.

Most of my working life has been spent teaching biology and everywhere that I have taught – mainly in England, but also in Kenya and America – I have coached runners. When my school athletes left school I continued to coach the keener ones and that led me on to picking up and coaching a number of other athletes. In the last ten years I have coached nearly twenty international distance runners. Between them they have won national titles at every level – English schools, British Universities, National Junior and Senior cross-country titles, AAA championships on the track and on the road, at every distance from the 1500metres to the marathon, and competed in the Olympic, European and Commonwealth Games as well as the World Track and Field and the World Cross-Country championships.

Of all those athletes, Richard Nerurkar stands out, for I learned at least as much from him as he learned from me. I started advising Richard in 1987, when he was leaving Oxford and going to Harvard. In 1989 he moved to Marlborough and took up a part-time teaching job at the boarding school of that name, where I had been teaching for fifteen years. This was the beginning of an unforgettable ten-year period in which Richard became Britain's leading long-distance runner. He became national champion at 10000m and later at the marathon. He won the national cross-country title three times, and led the British team to a medal in the World Championships. He finished fifth in the 1996 Olympic marathon and in 1993 he became the first British marathon runner to win a major title for nineteen years, when he won the World Cup marathon in San Sebastian.

To achieve these goals Richard put everything into his running, going up to 140 miles a week. Every winter we went to Kenya for altitude training and in most summers we went to Font Romeu in the Pyrenees for more altitude training. We also trained in Albuquerque, Boulder, and St. Moritz (all high altitude venues), in Florida, Finland, Greece, Italy, Japan, Mexico, Sweden and South Africa, either for the altitude benefits or for heat acclimatisation (yes, it's a tough life!). In those training camps we met most of the world's leading distance coaches and their athletes, and found out as much as possible about their methods. We talked to experts in nutrition, exercise physiology, weight training and sports psychology. We tried to learn about everything which was relevant to our purpose – how to develop Richard's potential as far as possible without using drugs or getting him injured. Although an injury eventually forced him to retire at the age of thirty-six, a few months short of competing in his third Olympics, I take pride in the fact that he was able to compete successfully at international level every year for ten years, usually as British number one. His best performances, apart from the World Cup win, included a 2 hr 08:36 marathon, a half marathon in 61:06 and a 10000m in 27:40.0.

When I stopped competing at the highest level I started to write books about running and that too has been going on for more than thirty years. I started writing for *Jogging* magazine when it first came out in 1978, stayed with it when it got fitter and became *Running* magazine and stayed again when it was taken over by *Runner's World.* This has brought me into contact with a world of running quite different from the elite world I already knew, but the principles of training remain exactly the same.

Personal stuff: Sue

I started running nearly forty years ago, mainly to get my figure back after our son was born. I trained with our friend Mary Rand, the Olympic long jump champion of 1964, who had had a baby a few weeks earlier, and joined her athletic club, London Olympiades. The first part of my career lasted only five years; I competed for my club at track and cross-country, won a national title for race-walking and got down to 4 mins 40-something for the 1500m. The high point of that part of my career was finishing 7th in the National cross-country in 1964. After our twins were born in 1970 I didn't start running again, apart from the occasional jog, until they were sixteen. However, having a strong interest in sport, I have always been involved with Bruce's coaching, holding the watch, getting to know the athletes, helping out in training camps. When we were working with Richard I took a sports massage course, so that he could get massage regularly after races or hard training sessions.

I was well into my forties when I got back to running regularly and almost immediately I ran into a problem. The more I ran, the more tired I got, so eventually I went to the doctor and was found to be seriously anaemic. A few weeks on a course of iron tablets had a transforming effect. The feeling of tiredness disappeared and the speed of my running increased enormously; it is a lesson I have never forgotten.

The next thing which gave my running a boost was the arrival in Marlborough of Richard Nerurkar. He would often do a run of ten miles or more in the mornings, when Bruce was teaching, and I used to go with him on my mountain bike, carrying spare clothing and a drink. Trying to keep up with him on hilly downland runs was totally exhausting, but it had a terrific effect on my fitness! I was adding two or three hours of strenuous cycling to my normal twenty miles a week of running, and as a result my times improved dramatically. My time for 10k came down with a jump from 48 minutes to 44 minutes.

The next thing was that we started going regularly to altitude training camps with Richard, and there was plenty of time for running – in fact, in those remote places, there is not much else to do! I learnt that, given time, I could handle much more running than I had thought possible, even at fifty. Whereas I might be running twenty miles a week at home, maybe thirty in a hard week, I was able to cope with fifty miles a week in a training camp. I found running at altitude very hard work, but when I came down, the effects were remarkable. Running a ten-mile race shortly after our return from Kenya, I improved my PB from 71 minutes to 68 minutes, at the age of 53. Whereas my first attempt at the marathon had resulted in a struggling 4 hr 45 at the age of 46, I improved to 3 hr 25 in my mid-fifties, and ran a half marathon in 90 minutes when I was 57. The only thing I regret was never quite breaking 40 minutes for 10k.

At each phase of life, different things take priority. When we were both heavily involved with coaching I was able to run a lot. Now we are older and not travelling to training camps, running is lower on the agenda. I run to keep fit and to keep my weight down. Golf, gardening and grandchildren take up more time – but I know what it is to be a runner.

Why a special book for over-forties?

We coach athletes by their ability, not by their age or sex. If a person wants to run a two-and a half hour marathon it is going to require at least seventy miles of running a week, maybe more. However, there are great differences in the approach to running taken by someone of forty as against someone of twenty. If the twenty-year-old is ambitious, he or she* will be aiming at County and National levels of competition. The young runner will be aiming for continuous improvement and increasing amounts of training, to match the higher standards. The over-forty runner is also aiming to get fit and run fast and he* may even wish to go on to veteran international events, but our goal is to reach a plateau of fitness and then stay there for as as long as possible.

The other reason is one of safety. The twenty-year-old can get away with things. She* can neglect her warm-down, miss a few days training, eat badly and still rise to the occasion.

The forty-year-old needs to be more thorough in warming-up and warming-down. On the other hand, the older runner has more mental endurance and often more physical endurance as well. He can cope with greater training mileages than the twenty-year-old. When Orde Wingate was picking his men, the Chindits, to fight in the Burmese jungle, he would take no one under thirty, because in his view they lacked the necessary stamina. Older runners may be slower, but they are tougher.

Apologies are due to those who have already been running for twenty-five years. Parts of this book will seem blindingly obvious, so please skip them. Remember that some of our readers will not know the first thing about running and will also know very little about how their bodies work.

---

* We are not going to write 'he or she' all the way through the book and we are not going to demean the runner by referring to him or her as 'it'. From now on 'he' can be taken to mean 'he or she' and 'she' can be taken to mean 'she or he'.

Birmingham
National City of
sport
Birmingham
National City of
sport
Alexander
Stadium
13-15 July
Norwich Union World Athletics
A60
A50
A40
A22

CHAPTER ONE:
Age and performance

"You are old, Father William, the young man said,
and your hair has become very white,
and yet you incessantly stand on your head,
do you think, at your age, it is right?"

LEWIS CARROLL

There was a time when a sportsman of any kind was considered too old at 28, over the top at 30. "Ageing legs", the commentators would say, knowingly. Sport was alright for young people and students, but certainly too frivolous for anyone over thirty, and downright irresponsible for a family man. The older you got, the less exercise was recommended.

These prophecies were, of course, self-fulfilling. We say we are too old, so we stop taking exercise, so we become less fit, so we cannot do as much. How things have changed! Nowadays the family man is being urged to take more exercise, cut down on his cholesterol intake and reduce his waistline, for the sake of his heart.

The first question people will ask is: am I too old to take up running? The answer to that is that you are never too old, though it must be said that the number of ninety-year-olds in competition is pretty small. What they are really asking is: Is it too late? Can I still hope to perform as well as I did when I was 18?

Don't worry! The world is full of examples of what can be done; some of them you will come across in this book. The seventy-year-old weight-lifter is stronger than the average thirty-year-old, the seventy-year-old ballet dancer is more flexible than the average thirty-year-old and the fit seventy-year-old runner will outrun the majority of thirty-year-olds at any distance over a mile. The 70-year-old Steve Charlton recently ran 10 kilometres in under 38 minutes, which would put him in the top 10% of most races in Britain or North America.

Such people owe their achievements not to the fact that they were outstanding when they were younger but to the fact that they have continued to practise the activity they enjoy.

It's easier for those who have been famous, because society tolerates them, even celebrates them; we can recall Jean Borotra and Kitty Godfrey playing tennis into their nineties, or Gene Sarazen teeing off at Augusta in the Master's. For those who are less distinguished, though, it sometimes requires moral courage, and this book is designed to reinforce that courage.

When we are young, we feel immortal and in a sense we are, because our cells renew themselves constantly. As we get older, the rate of cell division slows down, there is a loss of elasticity and some tissues perform less efficiently (see Chapter 2). The questions we need to look at are:

- How early do these changes set in?
- Is there anything we can do to reverse the process?
- What level of performance can we expect at a certain age?

Athletics has the advantage of being completely measurable, so we can see just what is happening. Having been a teacher for thirty years, Bruce has seen that in our civilization, people reach their physical peak between the ages of 16 and 18, and from then on their physical condition depends on their physical activity. Former pupils who come back a year or two after leaving school are already less fit, unless they have got into active sport. One of the spin-offs from the Vietnam war was that American surgeons had the opportunity of examining a lot of young corpses, and they found that most of those in the 19–21 age group already showed signs of degeneration, in the sense of increased fat storage and higher fat levels in the blood.

Am I too old to start?

Nigel Stuart-Thorn took up running at the age of 45. Twenty-five years later he is still running two thousand miles a year and racing almost every weekend. Last year he won the over-65 category in the French half-marathon championships, in 90:13.

For those who take up regular training, it is quite different. We can look at records and see that it is possible to remain at the very highest level up to the age of 35, if not further, as long as you have the motivaton to train properly. Linford Christie and Merlene Ottey showed that this is true for the sprints. In the longer distances, we can quote the examples of Carlos Lopes winning the World cross-country title and the Olympic marathon at the age of 37 and Eamonn Coghlan running a sub-four-minute mile at the age of 40. The message we can take from this is that it is possible to reverse most of the effects of ageing by taking the right kind of exercise.

What are the signs of ageing? By the late thirties, and sometimes as early as thirty, we can see the following:

- increasing weight
- thickening waistline
- declining strength
- poor posture
- lack of vigour
- loss of flexibility
- slower movements
- breathlessness
- lack of stamina
- thinning hair
- wrinkles

These outward signs are often accompanied by a general feeling of heaviness and malaise, sleeplessness and loss of appetite. Almost all of these things can be reversed by exercise:

- Your weight and your waistline will be brought down by burning up more calories per week and by sensible eating.
- Your muscular strength will improve rapidly with training.
- As your abdominal and back muscles get stronger and your fat declines, your posture will improve.
- The confidence and sense of well-being which come from being fit will make you more vigorous.
- Flexibility can be improved by regular stretching exercises.
- With less weight to carry and with increased fitness and strength, you will move faster and more easily.
- Training brings a big improvement in oxygen intake. You will still get breathless when training hard, but you will be able to cope easily with ordinary life.
- The increase in your powers of endurance will surprise you. Those who couldn't jog a mile can become fit enough to run a 26-mile marathon.

This still leaves us with the thinning hair and the wrinkles, but somehow, when you are fit healthy and happy about your body, they don't seem to matter as much.

To get an idea of what can be achieved by dedicated over-forty athletes, look at Table 1 below, which shows the current world records for over-forty men* and the Olympic winning performances for 1928, in the standard running events.

Table 1: Men's track records

Distance	1928 Gold	2001 over-40 record
100m	10.8	10.6
200m	21.8	21.86
400m	47.8	48.1
800m	1:51.8	1:51.25
1500m	3:53.2	3:46.7
5000m	14:38.0	13:45.6
10000m	30:18.8	28:30.88
Marathon	2 hr 32:57	2 hr 10:42

In 1928, the athletes were mostly university students in their twenties. These performances were the peak of physical achievement in their day. The best of today's over-forties have equalled or surpassed these standards. The four-minute mile was considered impossible until Roger Bannister did it in 1954, but now it's been done by a veteran. In the longer events, where modern training has really paid off, the achievements of today's best veterans surpass the runs of 'immortals' like Nurmi and Zatopek, and in the marathon the over-40 record is superior to Frank Shorter's 1972 Olympic winning time.

We can give you one more good example of what the older runner can achieve. Keith Anderson, when he was 31, was an overweight chef, with a demanding job, smoking 25 cigarettes a day. Ten years later, at the age of 41, he was marching into the Commonwealth Games stadium in Kuala Lumpur, as a member of the England marathon team. He went on to finish ninth in the marathon, the second of the six British runners.

Keith Anderson

These figures give you an idea of what can be achieved, at the highest level. We are not asking you to out-perform Zatopek or Shorter, just to make an improvement in your own personal level of fitness – and it can be done! The files are bulging with letters

* No comparisons have been made for women, because, with one exception, there were no events for women longer than 100m before WWII. It is worth noticing that Podkopayeva's world over-40 best for the 800m, 1:59.25, is superior to the 1968 winning Olympic time.

from men and women who have taken up the sport later in life. Not only have their health and fitness improved enormously, they have learned to savour life. It is hard to explain to an unfit person how much more alive you feel when you are really fit and healthy – it has to be experienced.

Bruce running in 1962...

...and 1989

How much does performance decline with age?

However hard you train, there will come a time when your racing speed will get slower.

BRUCE: "I have an exact record of every race from the age of 20, when I left the Army, to the age of 32, when I retired from international competition. I started competing again as a veteran at the age of 43, doing the *Sunday Times* Fun Run, and from then on I have a pretty continuous set of results, mostly over distances from 4k to the half marathon.

"In the *Sunday Times* Fun Run, held over the same four kilometre course at the same time of year, I slowed from 12:20 to 13:20 over a ten year period (from age 43 to 53). This represents 15 seconds per kilometre over 10 years, or 1.5 seconds/km/year. At the 5000m, my best racing distance, I was consistently around the 13:40–13:45 mark from 1960 to 1967, when I was just 32. Thirty-one years later I ran 17:40 for a 5k road course, a fall-off of 240 seconds, which represents 48 seconds per kilometre, which comes out at 1.5 seconds/km/year. Over 10000m, I ran 28:40 in 1967 and 32:30 at the age of fifty, some eighteen years later. This fall-off of 230 seconds, or 23 seconds per kilometre over 18 years, comes out at 1.3 seconds/km/year.

SUE: "My pattern was completely different. I started road running when I was 46, but I wasn't training very hard, so when I got into a harder training regime, my times improved a lot, in spite of getting older. The performances went up and down more in line with how hard I was training, rather than with increasing age. At 42, I ran about 20 minutes for the *Sunday Times* 4k, untrained, 17:00 at the age of 48, after a year of good training, and 16:20 two years later, when I was 50. Similarly, when training hard for the Centenary Boston Marathon in 1996, at the age of 54, I ran my fastest 10k for five years and ran 90:30 for the half marathon, equalling my best time of five years earlier."

Of course these are just personal results, and as we know, in any one year you may get a particularly good run, whereas another year you may have a bit of an injury, or you may run your best race when the wind is blowing hard.

> **"The pleasures and rewards of running are immeasurably greater for me at 46 than they were at 16 or 26. That is one of the most important and surprising discoveries of my middle life."**
>
> **ROGER ROBINSON**, HEROES AND SPARROWS, 1986

Fig. 1 shows the patterns of decline in two men who were good runners in their twenties and thirties and have gone on into over-forty competition. For Mick McGeoch we have year-on-year best times for 5000m, and for John Collins we have best performances in five-year age-bands, at 5k and 10k. There are fluctuations, which can be put down to fitness, injury or weather conditions, but overall, they both show a decline of about 1.5 secs/km/yr.

Fig. 1

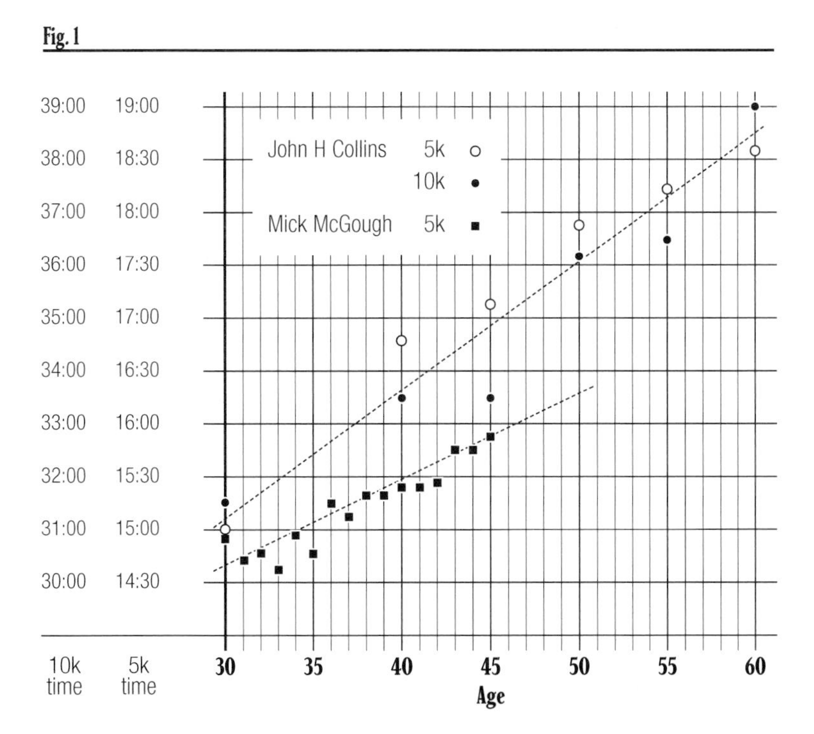

Different strokes

We started out with some pretty definite ideas on this topic. However, before starting on this book, we thought it would be a good idea to ask other over-forties for their experiences and their race results over the years – something which had not been done before. We put out an appeal through the newsletters and websites of the various veteran associations.and had almost two hundred replies within a few weeks.

The results were very illuminating – and totally confusing. There seem to be as many different patterns as there are individuals. Some have started at the age of nine, some at sixty-nine. Some have had a successful running career and then declined, while others have come from nowhere to become top-class veterans. Some have started out as sprinters and finished up as marathoners, others have gone the other way.

What was really striking was the way in which people who had been running on and off for years could show improvement and set personal bests in their fifties and even in their sixties. Take my friend Ted Townsend for example. Ted started running when he was 35, and before the age of 40 posted a respectable series of times – 41 minutes for the 10k and 1 hr 45 for the half marathon – on the basis of training hard two or three times a week. As he got older, he trained less hard but more often, and his times actually got better. At 45 he set a PB of 38:57 for the 10k and got his half marathon down to 1 hr 29 and as an over-50 he not only equalled his 1 hr 29 PB for a half marathon, he set a personal best for the marathon of 3 hr 24, forty minutes faster than he had been able to run in his thirties.

The new-wave runner

When someone takes up running for the first time, or comes back to it after a very long break, he or she will improve very quickly to start with – maybe five to ten seconds per mile (three to six secs per km.) per year, which means knocking a minute off the 10k time. After the second year this graph of improvement will start to level off, and eventually the graph of improvement due to training will collide with the graph of deterioration due to age (see Fig. 3). For a while you may be able to stay on a plateau, by training harder or by moving up to different events, but a time will come when you have to accept that your times are going to get slower rather than faster. This is where you have to change your outlook.

In Figs. 2 and 3 we see the typical pattern of runners who come to the sport later in life. With Gareth Jones (see below) we have yearly best performances at 10k, and with Richard Cashmore (see below right) we have best times for the marathon. Since Richard was racing five or six marathons every year in his early years, we get a more even curve here than in the later period where he only raced once or twice a year.

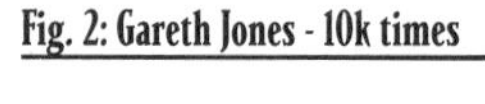
Fig. 2: Gareth Jones - 10k times

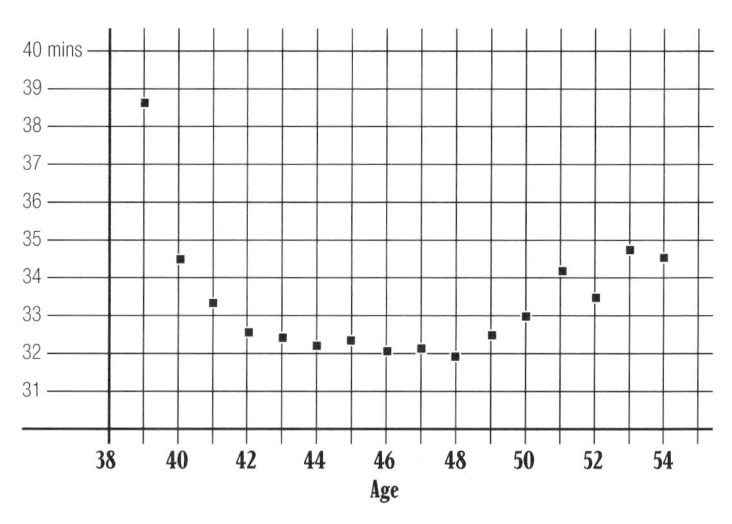

The main points here are:

- Whatever your age, it takes about five years from getting started to reaching lifetime bests.
- By far the biggest improvement is made in the first couple of years.
- If you get the training right, performances for the late starter can go on improving into your late forties and even early fifties.

It must be said that both these runners are highly talented. We have chosen them because they have accurate long-term records, but the principles would apply equally to a fifty-minute 10k runner or a four-and-a-half-hour marathon runner.

We can get an even better idea of how people slow down by taking the average from a large number of people.

The British Veterans Federation compiles Merit Tables, based on many performances over the whole age range. In the 5000m we find that the Grade One standard falls by 2:42 between the ages of 40 and 60. This drop of 32 seconds per kilometre over 20 years gives us 1.6 secs/km/year. Between the ages of 60 and 70 the decline in performance is more rapid – 2.4 secs/km/year. It is hard to extrapolate much further than that, because there are not many over-seventies clocking up serious performances, but the patterns are very consistent. The difference between the men's world best for 5000m, from 40 to 65, is almost three minutes – which is 36 secs/km over 25 years, or 1.4 secs/km/year, but there is a very big fall-off, two minutes, between the over-65 and the over-70 world record, which represents a decline of 4.8 secs/km/yr.

Fig. 3: Richard Cashmore - Marathon times

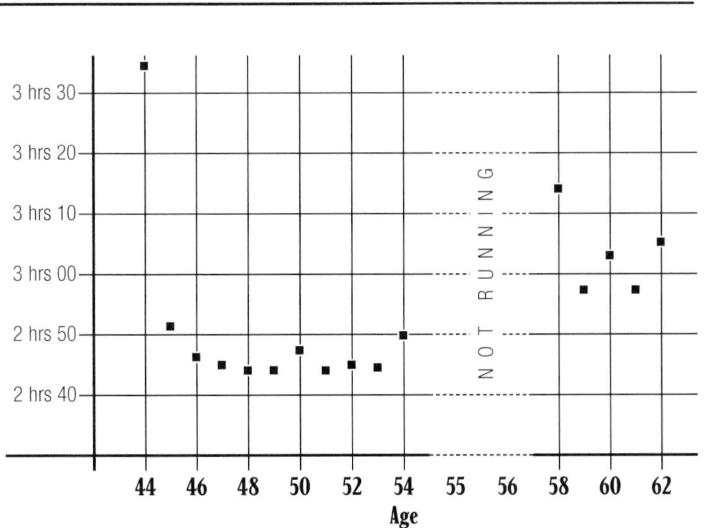

Using both the tables for the men's 10km we find that after the age of 60 the decline is more like 4 secs/km/year. However, with increasing numbers of serious athletes running in their sixties and seventies we would expect to find that this decline is not so rapid – and since we started this book, Ed Whitlock (see box p.26) has improved the over-70 10k record to an amazing 38:04. This is 3 mins 50 secs slower than the over-60 record, which is a decline of only 2.3 secs/km/yr.

The figures for women follow much the same pattern, but since they run more slowly, the decline in seconds/km/year is slightly greater. In the 5000metres, we find that the decline is a little over 2 seconds per km/year, and at 10000m about 2.5 secs/km/year over the 40–60 range. After that, we really cannot be accurate, because the number of runners is not great enough.

Not surprisingly, we find that those who train the hardest suffer the least decline in performance. Pat Gallagher (see p.60), who has been training hard since her late thirties, is an excellent example of this. As a W35 she ran 17:08 for 5000m, and as a W50 she ran 18:22 – a decline of only 74 seconds, which works out at fractionally under 1 second per kilometre per year, and her times at 1500m and 10k show a similar pattern.

There is still plenty of room for improvement in the over-90 and over 100 age group records. In the recent World Veterans Championships in Brisbane, the 101-year-old Australian Les Ames covered the 100m in 70 seconds and the 1500m in just under 20 minutes. It is only when we get a number of top class runners, male and female, carrying on into their seventies and eighties and competing against one another, that we will find out what the human body really can do. Until then, we must still say, as Dr. Johnson said about the dog walking on his hind legs: "the wonder is not that they do it well, but that they do it at all!"

> **"I thought I would tell you, my life was going nowhere, but since jogging came along I have had 25 years of joy. It's been heaven. I love running and I love watching it. I've run in places I never thought I would see."**
>
> **FRANK COPPING,** 77

The mental approach

Before starting on a running programme, you must have a clear idea of what your goals are. As we have learned from the letters we have received, there are many different reasons for running, and so the same training will not suit everybody. Some would say that a veteran runner is one who is no longer improving, but that is by no means the case. Someone who takes up the sport at 46 may go on getting better up to the age of 49 and then, approaching the age of fifty, may realise that he is ready to step into the leading ranks of over-fifty runners. From being either a has-been or a never-was, he has the prospect of winning prizes, running in international competitions, maybe representing his country.

Even without taking age into account, there are at least three main categories of runner:

- **elite competitors:** these people are at the top of the age-group rankings and they are prepared to train as hard as possible to achieve their goals.
- **club runners:** these people are also competitors, but they are not aiming for the very top. They will have particular events to train for at different times of the year – maybe a spring or autumn marathon, some track races in the summer, some inter-club relay events. Their main concern is staying fit and being able to perform respectably.
- **non-competitive runners:** these people run either because they enjoy running or because it is their chosen way of keeping fit and healthy.

The mental approach dictates the schedules you embark on and your attitude to them.

For example, suppose that we have a period of really bad weather in January. The elite runner will carry on with his training. If he can't do his repetition kilometres on the road he will go to the nearest track and do them there. If the track is closed he will drive to a gym and do them on a treadmill. The club runner will not be prepared to give up the extra time, so he will just put on an extra layer of clothing and go out for a short run in the snow. The "keep-fit" runner will be on a programme which includes activities other than running, like swimming or weight training, so he can concentrate on the indoor activities and save the running until the weather improves.

If you have just taken up running, you may start off as the 'non-competitive' type, then get drawn into a club, and maybe even become an elite runner. If you have been running seriously for twenty years before reaching veteran status, you may well move the other way, competing seriously in the first few years, then being satisfied with club-level competition and later on concentrating mainly on keeping fit and just having the occasional race for fun.

The 'new wave' runner has an entirely different attitude to the long-time runner. The newcomer to the sport is discovering for the first time all the sensations of feeling fit, running fast, passing people in races. He has all the enthusiasm of the eighteen-year-old inside a forty-year-old body. This can sometimes be dangerous, but it can also lead to great achievements.

For this reason our rule of thumb is that the athlete should train according to ability and ambition rather than age or sex. If somebody has improved, say, from a 5 minute 1500m to 4:50, and wants to get better, the same principles apply whether we are dealing with a 15-year-old boy, a 40-year-old woman or a 50-year-old man.

Having said that, there are differences in training, depending on the athlete's background. The long-time runner already has thousands of miles of training behind him. It will take him less time to move up to harder training than the newcomer who has never trained at that level.

The Ulysses factor

There are plenty of good reasons to run, but there are also powerful forces pushing in the other direction. What is life if we cannot enjoy it? Are not good food and good drink inseparable from good company? With air pollution, radiation, food additives and global warming, our chances of survival are slim, so why not just eat, drink and be merry?

BRUCE: "Why not? I eat well, drink moderately, sing quite a lot and am frequently merry. The point is that being a runner I can work off the food and the alcohol without putting on weight. I can enjoy life more and do more because I am healthy. Running should add to your life, not diminish it."

Other insidious remarks are along the lines of: "You should act your age!" and "Exercise can do more harm that good." Like all propaganda, this is incomplete truth. The fact that over twenty years one or two people have died while running the London Marathon does not mean that running kills you. Yachtsmen are more likely to drown than non-sailors and climbers are more likely to have climbing accidents than non-climbers. Overweight joggers occasionally die while jogging.

What is overlooked is the large number of non-exercisers who die whilst non-exercising. Bed is a dangerous place to be – a lot of people die in bed.

We are not immortal. We are all affected by the ageing process and it would be stupid to ignore this, but that does not mean we cannot slow it down. Tennyson's words, from his poem *Ulysses*, sum it up:

"Though much is taken, much abides, and though
We are not now that strength which in old days
Moved earth and heaven, that which we are, we are:
One equal temper of heroic hearts,
Made weak by time and fate, but strong in will
To strive, to seek, to find and not to yield."

Fine words, but where do they get us? They might get us to take the long view, for a start, and they might stimulate that sense of purpose and challenge without which nothing is achieved. Working or training, without a sense of purpose, is drudgery. If you have nothing left to live for, you might as well die. If you are forty when reading this, you probably have more than half your life ahead of you. If you are going to live a long time you had better take care of yourself.

Fitness is not the same as health. Being fit will not protect you against every known disease, but it will shift the balance onto the credit side. It is now proven that those who exercise regularly are much less likely to suffer from the cardiovascular diseases such as strokes and heart attacks. The extra strength and flexibility which comes from fitness will protect you against the little accidents which tend to ambush us in middle age – the strained back, the twisted ankle.

What fitness gives us is a safety margin, a reserve of vitality which enables us to cope with emergencies. You come back on the last train from London. You are four miles from home, the car won't start and it's starting to snow. In a situation like this, someone who is not physically robust might feel a bit panic-stricken. The breaking of one link in the chain of normal events releases a flood of irrational fears.

This is where the Ulysses factor comes in. The man or woman who has physical confidence reacts to a stressful situation in a positive way. You have been through stressful situations before, maybe in a race, on a mountainside, in a forest. You know you can cope, so you simply look around for the best solution – which in this case is an easy jog or a brisk walk home – not stressful, just a good bit of exercise – end of story.

Ten reasons for running

Running keeps your weight down
Running makes you fitter
Running lowers your cholesterol level
Running lowers your blood pressure
Running gives you confidence
Running helps you live longer
Running improves your bone density
Running gives you great legs
Running makes you feel better
Running makes you look better

Being able to cope with stress, having a reserve of energy, these are justifications for being a runner, but they are not the real reasons. The reasons should be that we enjoy the exercise, we enjoy being fit and we enjoy a challenge. Ulysses stayed strong enough to bend the bow.

Achieving perfection

Man is a competitive animal. We are descended from those who were the quickest off the mark, the handiest with the flint axe – and the best at running away in defeat. Running in races gives us a perfect outlet for our competitive spirit. We can fight as hard as we want, beat our opponents, give them a thrashing, and yet nobody need get hurt.

In the early years of veteran competition you will find that the spirit of rivalry burns every bit as strongly as it does amongst the twenty-somethings. People who never won anything in the past can realise their dreams of winning medals and putting on an England vest. However, the longer you stay in the veteran ranks, the more you will find that your opponents become old friends. The outcome is often decided by who is injured or who has just got over an injury.

So when you turn up for a local road race and you find yourself alongside the man who beat you for the county junior title when you were nineteen, you don't think: "Here's that old git come to spoil my chances again". You should be thinking: "that's good, here is someone I can run with, who can help me achieve my goal." Your real enemy is time and you are both fugitives from the winged chariot. What is more likely, of course, is that you will look on him as a rival and push yourself a bit harder than usual. No one has put it better than the late George Sheehan, who said: "Of course we are not really competing against each other – we are all witnesses to each others achievements – but dammit, I hate to get beaten by a witness in my own age group!"

What should happen is that, like Buddhists, the older we get, the closer our attitudes move towards perfection. The ninety-year-old runner is concerned with running smoothly and consistently; he is not going to be worried about competition (because he's outlived them all!) and that should always be our attitude.

Martin Rees

age: **48** occupation: **steel worker**

To be a successful sportsman in South Wales you have to be really good. It may be the cradle of Welsh rugby, but it also produces such runners as Steve Jones, who set a British marathon record of 2 hr 07:13 seconds back in 1985, Christian Stephenson and Steve Brace. Martin Rees runs for Swansea Harriers. He is a steel worker at the Port Talbot plant – a demanding job. For years he worked eight-hour shifts, rotating every few days from the Early to the Late to the Night shift, so that the sleep pattern was constantly changing. He regularly cycled to work – half an hour each way – which kept him lean and fit, but he didn't get into running until 1991, when he was 38.

A friend persuaded him to take part in a local 10k road race, and he ran it in 44 minutes – promising but unremarkable. He then tried a ten mile race and coped with that with little trouble. Finding that he had a natural talent for the sport he joined Swansea and started training. His times improved steadily and each year he trained a bit harder. When he turned forty he was winning most of the veteran prizes in local races and soon moved into National class as a veteran. He won national titles on the road in His best times were mostly done at the age of 44 – 14:20 secs for 5k, 49:23 for ten miles and 65:37 for the half marathon – but at the age of 47 he clocked 30:25 for 10k, only just outside the PB of 30:12 he ran four years earlier, and now, at 48, he seems to be running as fast as ever over the longer distances. So far he has only attempted two marathons, with a best of 2 hr 23 which does not really satisfy him, so we can expect one or two more PBs before he turns 50.

The training which has enabled him to reach this level is fairly conventional, but tough: "In the autumn I put in three months of 100 miles a week and the rest of the year I run about 70-75 miles a week, running as I feel, really. I also cycle to work and back, thirty minutes each way. I like to put in a tempo run once a week and also a speed session, but if I am tired I just go easy. I very rarely do track work, but I get a lot of strength from running on hills."

M40
VETERANS RELAYS 98
8
THE RUNNERS SHOP

CHAPTER TWO

The human machine

"If I'd known I was going to live this long,
I'd have taken better care of myself!"

NEW ORLEANS JAZZ MUSICIAN **EUBIE BLAKE**
ON REACHING HIS 100TH BIRTHDAY

The human body can be compared to a machine – it has fuel, an air intake, lots of small motors, a body and a transmission system. However, it is greater than a machine, because it is self-regulating and self-repairing.

The fuel

The body normally obtains its energy by burning a mixture of fats and carbohydrates, but it can also burn alcohol, and in cases of extreme starvation it will burn protein. The energy production process, known as respiration, takes place in every living cell. As the hydrocarbon units are split up, they are combined with oxygen, so that the end-products are water, carbon dioxide and energy. The energy is used to make ATP (adenosine triphosphate), which can then be used for any process in the cell which requires energy. The muscle cells need energy for muscular contraction, so that is where most of the respiration goes on when we are running. Because oxygen is involved, it is called Aerobic Respiration.

Energy can be produced without the use of oxygen and the by-product of the breakdown of sugars is lactic acid (otherwise known as blood lactate). This substance is poisonous to the cells, and unless oxygen is available to oxidise away

Alison Fletcher – silver medallist in the World Veterans championships

the lactic acid, the muscles will be unable to work. The amount of oxygen needed to get rid of the lactic acid is known as 'oxygen debt'.

The air intake

The air is drawn into the lungs, via the nose and mouth, by the action of the chest muscles and the diaphragm. In the lungs, an exchange of gases takes place. Blood pumped from the heart passes in tiny capillary blood vessels through the thin walls of the alveoli, which are the ultimate subdivisions of the lung chambers. In a second or two the red blood cells become fully saturated with oxygen, giving up the carbon dioxide which they were carrying. The haemoglobin in the red cells has a very strong affinity for oxygen, so it carries oxygen to all the cells of the bodies, via the arteries, the arterioles and the capillaries. The rate at which it delivers the oxygen depends largely on the capacity of the pump, which is the heart. The heart muscle is very elastic, and it can increase the stroke volume (the volume of blood pumped at each beat) as well as the rate of the heart beat.

The motors

Movement is brought about by the contraction of muscle fibres. The fibres are arranged in bundles and unless you are making a huge effort, not all the fibres in a bundle are brought into action at the same time. Part of the training process is 'educating' the muscles, so that when necessary all the muscle fibres can be recruited at the same time. Conversely, the lower the proportion of fibres which are working, the less fuel and oxygen are used, so part of the skill of running lies in running efficiently and economically, using only the essential muscles.

The transmission

The force from the contracting muscles pulls on the tendons, which are attached to movable bones. When the front part of the foot is in contact with the ground, the contraction of extensor muscles around the hip, knee and ankle raises the heel and the whole body. At the same time the back leg is being brought through from behind and the centre of gravity is moving forwards. Other muscles are contracting so as to keep the non-moving parts of the body rigid. If you did not have strong back muscles, your chest would be pulled forwards as your knee is brought up. It is because the human body is not rigid like a car that you need to have a strong all-round muscular system.

The suspension

As your front foot hits the ground there is an impact shock. If you are over-striding this may actually slow you down, but in any case there is a shock in a vertical plane which has to be absorbed. We have built-in 'springs' in the arches of our feet and in elastic tendons in ankle and knee, which are compressed slightly when your foot plants and then return the energy so that you bounce a little. This pogo-stick effect is shown to perfection in the kangaroo, but even in humans it makes the body's running action more efficient. This is the reason why you need to get your stride length just right for each speed. The inexperienced runner has very few built-in shock absorbers and tends to slap the ground rather hard, while the experienced and stylish runner glides along with little apparent effort.

Is there such a thing as a 'correct' foot action? The answer is that everyone is different. The faster you run, the more you tend to run on your toes, to get a long stride. It is very difficult to change your stride length – so you are better off choosing the distance which best suits your stride.

The chassis

As in a car, the chassis tends to slow you down. If you have a heavy chassis powered by a small engine you cannot go very fast. A reduction of 10% in weight will give you a 10% increase in speed, so if a 60kg person loses 6kg, he can expect to improve by 10%, which is 36 seconds a mile for a six-minute miler.

Because a bit of weight loss brings a big improvement, it is tempting to think that a bigger weight loss will bring even more improvement, but this is not the case. Once your body fat is down to its safe limit (somewhere around 8% for men,

12% for women), extra weight loss can be damaging, either because you break down protein or because it affects your immune system.

The art of running

There is little in the way of skill or technique involved in distance running. Success depends on a combination of natural ability, training and mental attitude, and of these three, natural ability far outweighs the other two in deciding the results. we would say that success depends 80% on natural ability, with training making up at least 15% of the remainder, and mental attitude accounting for less than 5%. If you put two people of equal ability into a 10k race, with roughly equal amounts of training behind them, the highly motivated one, pushing himself really hard, might finish a minute ahead of the other, but probably not more than two minutes, which represents about 5% of the running time.

The body's potential may not emerge for quite a long time, if the person has not kept fit since their schooldays. Excess weight, carried as fat, not only makes running more difficult, it also causes people to overheat, so making them more uncomfortable and slowing them down.

Whether you are a 'natural sportsman' or not has nothing to do with it. The so-called natural sportsman always has good eyesight and good hand-eye co-ordination, but these factors have no bearing on running success. Some of the best runners are hopeless at ball games and have channelled their sporting ambition into the one thing they can do well, while others are good at ball games and could have excelled in a number of sports.

Fast or slow?

What does matter is muscle fibre type. The bundles of fibres which make up our muscles contain varying proportions of 'slow twitch' and 'fast twitch' fibes, as well as some which are intermediate and may by training become fast- or slow-twitch. Sprinters' muscles may contain over 75% of the fast twitch type, whereas the muscles of marathon runners are mostly of the slow twitch type.

Middle distance runners, who run 800m or 1500m on the track contain roughly equal amounts and by training may shift in one direction or the other, which explains why someone like Steve Ovett could perform well at 400m or in the half marathon. If you are a natural sprinter, with mostly fast-twitch fibres, you are never going to make a good long-distance runner, and vice-versa. There are two ways of finding out – either by having a muscle biopsy done or by trying a range of events in your first year. If you find that the shorter the distance you run, the better you do, then you should concentrate on short-distance events. If you have always been lacking in natural speed you probably have more slow-twitch fibres and should go for the longer events.

There are many other factors involved in that quality known as 'natural ability'. Body weight, relative to your height, is one of the most significant of these. Since running is simply a matter of carrying your own weight over a distance, it is obvious that that those who are light in weight have less to carry – and that makes a lot of difference. In horse-racing, carrying an extra seven pounds more or less has a marked effect on a horse's performance – and the horse may weigh five hundred pounds – so how much more it affects the way humans run.

A quick way of finding out where you stand is by working out your Body Mass Index. Divide your weight in kilos by your height in centimetres. A 60kg man who is 180cm in height would have a BMI of 60/180, which is 0.333 kg/cm. A short squat man, weighing 80kg and only 160cm tall would have a BMI of 0.5 kg/cm. Other things being equal, the lower the BMI, the easier it will be to run. However, a really skeletal underweight person would not be a good runner, because most of his weight would be bone, with no muscle to propel it.

An obvious factor here is how much fat you are carrying. Fat is literally dead weight, because it is not being used to hold you up or move you forward, as muscle is. Another parameter for measuring your efficiency as a runner is the measurement of your percentage of body fat. This can be estimated by taking pinches of skin in various places around the body and measuring the thickness with calipers. The simplest way is to take a pinch of skin in your midriff, just above your hip bone. Roughly speaking, if the pinch is 10 mm thick, you have 10% body fat; if it's 20mm thick, you have 20%, and so on. Good male runners have no more than 10% body fat, good female runners 13%, but within the population in general, figures of 20% for men and 25% for women are not uncommon.

If you have not taken exercise for years you may well be carrying extra fat, which makes it more difficult for you to run, and therefore hides your real ability. We have already mentioined Keith Anderson, but there is an even more dramatic example in the Irish-Canadian marathon runner, Pete Maher. Pete had been a good runner in his youth, but in his twenties he had taken to drink and ballooned up to carrying sixteen or seventeen stone on his six-foot frame. He was watching the World Championships marathon in a bar somewhere, and said to his mates: "I could do that, you know. I used to be a runner." Their replies were along the lines of: "In yer dreams. You couldn't run a hundred yards, you fat slob." Their comments stung him to such an extent that he stopped drinking, took up running again, and he not only made the Irish team for the next Olympics, he led the Olympic marathon field for about twenty miles.

However, even if you are fairly slim and long-legged, with a goodish proportion of slow-twitch fibres, there is no guarantee that you will be a good long-distance runner. What we cannot see are the mechanisms inside. First of all you need a robust skeletal system, with strong bones and joints, which can withstand the impact of running, supported by strong ligaments to hold the joints in place. You need strong muscles and tendons, with a rich blood supply. You need a good strong heart, healthy lungs and a good system of arteries and veins to carry the blood to the muscles and back again. At a deeper level still you need efficient cell chemistry for converting glucose into the energy the muscles require. You need a balanced and responsive hormone system, which will react to stress by pumping out the hormones your body needs to perform at a high level.

The more you go into the physiology of exercise, the more complex it becomes. Knowing a lot about it doesn't make you run any faster, but sometimes it helps to understand why certain types of training are recommended.

What do we mean by fitness?

Fitness really means 'suitablity'. It is very specific. A man who has the fitness to run a good 400m would not have the fitness to run a good marathon. A man who is fit for swimming would not be fit for mountain climbing. A man who is fit enough to run a marathon might find himself quite unfit for downhill skiing, and so on. However, we would probably agree that true fitness includes the following main points:

1. Not carrying a lot of fat.
2. Not getting breathless while walking fast uphill.
3. Able to maintain steady physical exercise for a couple of hours without needing to rest.
4. Not feeling stiff the morning after a day's exercise.
5. Being able to perform your chosen sport several times a week.

To these we might add the following, which might come under 'health', rather than 'fitness':

6. Having a good appetite.
7. Sleeping well and waking up refreshed.
8. No stiff joints or aching bones.
9. Having a full range of movement for normal activities.
10. Having enough strength to cope with everyday needs.

While we would expect that most runners would answer well to all these criteria, they would not define 'fitness' in the running sense. A thirty-minute 10k runner would give the same answers as a forty-five-minute runner, but that does not mean that they are equally fit.

What does a runner mean by 'fitness'?

When someone says to another runner: "Are you fit, then?", he means: "Are you as fit as you would like to be?", or "Are you at your best possible state of fitness for your event?"

The answer is almost invariably: "No, not really," quickly followed by a string of excuses (or 'reasons' as they are called when you are talking about yourself).

Ahmed Amraoui – hard training pushes back by years

Full fitness, to a sportsman or woman, means being able to perform his event to his maximum potential at that time, so unless you have had an unbroken period of hard training for the last three months, you are always going to be a little short of full fitness. Of course 'hard training' means different things to different people. If Bruce runs less than 30 miles in a week, he regards it as a poor week, and if over 40, it's a good week; an international runner would regard anything under 70 miles as being an easy week but for someone else, getting up to 20 miles a week for eight weeks in a row might represent seriously hard training.

Fitness is always relative, not absolute. When friends say to you: "Are you fit?", what they really mean is: "Are you at your normal/desired level of fitness?" If you are fit enough to run 10k in 45 minutes, that would be marvellous if your previous best was 48 minutes, but not so good if you are accustomed to running it in under 30 minutes.

Fitness is not like Virginity – either you have it or you don't – it is like standing on a moving staircase, on the down escalator. If you stand still, you go down, if you make a little effort you stay in the same place, but if you want to get to the top, you have to make a big effort.

Cross-country running is easier on the legs, but no less tough

The ageing machine

Richard Barrington has been running for 47 years, 16 of those as a veteran, doing track running, hurdling, cross-country, road and fell-running. His times, which used to be around 50 secs for 400m and 55 secs for 400m hurdles, are now around 60 and 66 seconds, but in those years he has seldom been injured. This must be due in part to his scientific background, which enables him to understand what is going on. Writing in the *Journal of Sport and Medicine*, 1988, his views can be summarised as follows:

"In the young body, damaged cells are replaced very quickly, whether they are muscle fibres or red blood cells. As we get older, this regeneration takes place more slowly. Cuts take longer to heal, bruises and strained muscles stay longer and new blood cells are formed more slowly. If we race or train hard, we feel tired for longer.

"Another change in the body is the loss of elasticity. The elastic protein fibres are gradually replaced by stronger but less elastic proteins. This has the effect of slowing leg speed. The slowdown is even more marked in sprinters, because over time the effect of years of training is to decrease the proportion of fast twitch fibres, with a increase in slow twitch fibres and inelastic connective tissue.

"A further effect comes directly from years of competition – the accumulation of scar tissue from previous injuries. Those who have competed for many years at one event pick up particular injuries – damaged ankles in triple jumpers, scarred hamstrings in sprinters, battered joints in road runners. This is where the 'new wave' runner, who starts injury-free, has an advantage over the 'old stager'. However, when it comes to running marathons the latter has the advantage of being pre-conditioned by earlier training, so is less likely to develop over-use injuries."

The problems of injury and how to deal with it are dealt with in Chapter 13, but the conclusions which Richard Barrington comes to cannot be stated too often:

1. Hard training produces some damage, which takes time to repair.
2. The older the athlete, the longer this takes.
3. A day or two of rest or easy running is needed to get over the effects of hard training.

The hormone story

The hormone system is a method of communication through which the body responds to changes. The hormones are chemicals carried in the blood, so they can affect several parts of the body at the same time. Some hormones are produced for a few minutes only, others over days and weeks. As runners, the first hormone we think of is adrenaline, the hormone of 'flight and fright' which has a big effect on performance. Adrenaline and noradrenaline bring about an increase in heart rate, a rise in blood pressure, an increase in the level of blood sugar and a diminished sense of pain. It is the production of adrenaline which enables us to perform much better in races than in training. It is the 'adrenaline rush' which makes race day exciting.

In response to training, however, other hormones are important. Growth hormone (GH) is vital in stimulating the processes of muscle repair and development, and one of the things which distinguishes the good athlete from the mediocre is the ability of the good athlete to produce high levels of GH – and thus cope with bigger training loads.

When we look at GH production at different ages, we find, not surprisingly, that the old are less responsive than the young. Researchers at the University of Colorado* measured the levels of a number of different hormones before and after exercise, comparing trained and untrained people of different ages.

* Silverman and Mazzeo, *Journal of Gerontology*, Vol. 51A, 1996

The strange case of **Ed Whitlock**

More or less everything we have written about inevitable slowing down appears to be contradicted by Ed Whitlock, a seventy-year-old English-born Canadian, who lives in Milton, Ontario. In October 2000 he ran 2 hr 52.50 for the Columbus,Ohio, Marathon, and it is a pretty safe bet that by the time this book is in print he will have become the first 70-year-old to run a marathon in under three hours. In the 2001 Wolrd Veterans Championships he won both the 5000 and the 10000m, the latter in a world's best time of 38 mins 4 seconds, and he's also run a half-marathon recently in 80 minutes.

Of course every runner would like to know his secret, but there is no secret. He doesn't take any magic potions – not even vitamin pills. He doesn't stretch, he doesn't do weights or cross-training and he doesn't do any quality running apart from his races. He continues to maintain a high mileage – running two to three hours a day, over 100 miles a week, something which none of us 'experts'would recommend. Laboratory tests showed just what one would expect from someone who can run those times – low body-fat and a VO_2 max of 52.8ml/kg/min.

Studies of his hormone levels and his haemoglobin showed nothing out of the ordinary. The answer lies in his attitude and in his family background. His mother lived to ninety-three, his father died in his eighties, and his father's brother lived to 107. It seems likely that Ed Whitlock is one of those people who ages very slowly, and that is why he doesn't break down or get injured, in spite of his volume of training.

Without those genes, he could not be the success he is, but the genes would not give him success if he didn't have the will to succeed, the desire to be the best he possibly can be.

He has the ability – he won a World Master's title at 1500m when he was 48 – he has the desire and he has found a training method which suits him. That's all you need.

The pre-exercise level of GH was between 1.0 and 1.4 units (ng/ml) in all the groups. After due precautions they were given an exercise test on a static cycle ergometer, working up to 'maximal exertion'. After exercise the GH level was 5.6 in untrained young men, but 21.9 in the trained group. In the middle-aged group (age around 45) the figures were 8.6 (untrained) and 19.0 (trained). Even in the elderly group (mid-sixties) the results were quite clear – the levels were 2.8 for the untrained and 11.3 for the trained group. This ability to produce Growth Hormone enables the trained men to respond better to stresses and traumas. Their capacity for growth and repair is much greater.

You will have noticed that even in the untrained men there was a big response to the exercise test – their problem was that this was the only time when they took any exercise! This group of researchers concluded that:

1. Training can increase the growth hormone response to exercise in the elderly.

2. This has the benefits of increasing lean muscle, decreasing fat percentage and increasing the capacity of the heart.

Their overall conclusion, looking at a number of different hormones, was that endurance training improved the capacity of the middle-aged and elderly to respond to "disruptions in homeostasis".

If we are looking at this question from the angle of: What is the best way to improve performance?, it is worth mentioning that growth hormone levels are not affected much unless the exercise is quite intense – at least up to Threshold level (ten-mile pace). To get a response from the body you have to stimulate it, and that means doing some of your training at a fast pace – at least 10k pace and preferably 5k pace.

This scientific evidence bears out what runners and coaches have always known – that you have to push yourself hard to produce an effect. At the same time, we have to avoid the breakdown caused by over-training, which is why we advise people to follow a recommended training schedule in the early stages and only to experiment when they have reached a high level of fitness. This is where a heart monitor comes in useful, because you can keep a close watch on your level of training.

However, we must always bear in mind that the best distance runners in the world, the Kenyans and Ethiopians, run faster than anybody without the benefit of scientific knowledge. The best way to get fitter and to find out if you are any good is to get out and start doing something.

Hormones and your sex life

When hormones are mentioned, sex is the first thing which comes to mind. You can blame almost anything on hormone levels when it comes to sex. We have all read horror stories about 'testosterone freaks' who raise their hormone levels to improve their weightlifting performance and then become uncontrollable sex maniacs. It is a fact that levels of both growth hormone and testosterone (male sex hormone) decline after the age of 40, and falling hormone levels often result in a loss of sex drive. However, recent research at the University of Newcastle, reported in *The Observer* (23rd May 2000) showed that the effects of ageing can be reversed by hard training, driving up the hormone levels and giving older men more sex drive. Men aged 55–65 who trained more than 40 miles a week were found in this study to have higher levels of both hormones than normal men of a similar age who did no regular exercise.. According to Pat Kendall-Taylor, the Professor of Endocrinology, the runners had four times the level of growth hormone and 25% more testosterone. This is not enough to turn old men into testosterone freaks, but it is enough to make a difference – once you have recovered from your run. Although the study was done on only two groups of ten, the results were statistically significant – and of course they tie up with what we have already pointed out about growth hormone.

The HRT story

By stimulating the production of growth hormone and testosterone, running is doing for men what Hormone Replacement Therapy does for women. Because HRT treatment has only been widely used in the past 20 years, there are still those who harbour doubts about it, but the effects on middle-aged women have been quite striking.By maintaining the levels of the female sex hormones after ovulation ceases, HRT keeps women biologically younger, which means that they feel better, look better, have more energy and run faster.

Helen Stokes

age: **44** started running at: **36** occupation: **part-time drama teacher, mother of three**
best performances: **10k** 44:45 **half marathon** 1hr 38 **marathon** 3 hr 38

"Most of the time my family think I am bonkers and that goes for most of my non-running friends too! What explanation can you offer, as a born-again runner, to those who can't relate to the satisfaction of sliding through mud, panting up hills or pounding the pavements in sub-zero temperatures?

"I tell people I started running to prevent me from beating my children and there is a grain of truth in that: childcare and housework have their joys, but for those who are achievement orientated the everyday tasks give little satisfaction. Going for a run is a self-contained activity; you go, you return and there is the accomplishment of having achieved something – and of course there is the flexibility of it being a solitary activity requiring no particular venue, which you can fit in at any time.

"I am in the fortunate position of counting amongst my friends some very good runners: the enthusiasm they have shown over the years for my paltry efforts has been immensely significant. If you are a capable runner you can do so much for those way behind you, just by showing an interest in their problems and their progress. I have never been made to feel that my achievements are unimportant and my 'triumphs' have been celebrated with the best of them.

"There have been interesting moments along the way; I've run in all sorts of places, from rural France to Central Park, New York. The most bizarre moment was the 'nettle sting' which turned out to be an adder bite. It cleared up with heavy doses of antibiotics, but I'm glad I didn't see the snake actually making contact! On the plus side, it always makes me smile when I win a prize, because it's unexpected. Last week I entered a race at the last minute, with no special training, and was first lady.

"I am proud that I can run quite well, but always wish that I was a bit fitter. I enjoy running with friends and sorting out my problems – I've discussed family problems, worked out lessons and debated the ordering of God's universe. When I see the more ancient ladies and gentlemen running the London marathon I am humbly impressed – and I hope to be there too."

CHAPTER THREE

A short history of running

"Sexual intercourse began in 1963, between the Lady Chatterly *trial and the Beatles' first LP."*

...wrote Philip Larkin. A similar fallacy holds that running started in America in the 1970s, between Fred Lebow's first New York Marathon and the publication of Jim Fixx's *The Complete Runner.*

Running and fighting are the world's two oldest sports. Bear cubs wrestle, rabbits run. In all societies, children have wrestled and run races, adolescents and young adults have competed for prestige. Undoubtedly, organised sport preceded written record by a long way, so we will never know when humans started racing, but my guess is that it was a very short time after man came down from the trees and started hunting on two legs – so that would be four million years ago. Humans are designed for running, and because running was essential for survival we are all descended from runners.

We know that the Olympic Games can be traced back to the 13th Century BC, and these were only one of a number of Games, which included the Pythian, Nemean and Isthmian Games. There is a fresco in Crete, dating from the time of King Minos (1600 BC) which shows a team of runners, three of them women, all, by their running action, distance runners.

In Ireland the Tailtean Games are said to have been founded in 1829 BC, which takes us back even further, and there are records of running being a part of ritual ceremonies in the Egypt of the Pharaohs.

The first sports report of a running event was written by Homer in the *Iliad*, when he describes a race under the walls of Troy. The race was part of the funeral games for Patroclus, put on by Achilles, who was himself renowned as an unbeatable runner. There were only three runners, Aias the Runner, son of Oileus, Antilochus, son of Nestor, and the wily Odysseus. The result was a win for the veteran Odysseus ("a relic of the past, but his old age is green"), who tucked right in behind Aias and then put in a winning burst just as Aias slipped on a pile of cow dung. Since then, things have not changed much.

BRUCE: "The ancestry of the sport was vividly brought home to me when I visited the Tarahumara Indians in Mexico. These people are a branch of the Apache nation who migrated into Northern Mexico about a thousand years ago. They now live in the mountains of the Sierra Madre Occidentale, West of Chihuahua, in small villages which have retained the customs of their ancestors. They mix little with the surrounding population and have retained their own language alongside the Spanish which everyone speaks."

Of these customs, the central one is the kick-ball race, which is a form of relay race between rival village teams, with four to six in a team. They use a wooden ball, about the size of a cricket ball, which is flicked forwards with the toes (they run in sandals), to the runner in front. The man who has flicked the ball then runs up to the front of the line. This is done on dirt roads which run up and down the valleys between the villages. The most remarkable thing about it is the distance. The standard race starts one day and finishes the next, so is up to 24 hours, and the big races can be up to 48 hours, running non-stop through the night, carrying flaming pine branches. The whole team has to keep running, with no substitutes allowed.

The races are taken very seriously. There is heavy betting beforehand. A race Bruce watched, thirty years ago, was preceded by several days of betting, mostly conducted in complete silence. A man puts out the money or the objects he wishes to wager in a pile on the ground and those who wish to bet against him place objects alongside until an agreement is reached.

Drug-taking is part of the event, using coca leaves and other natural stimulants to keep them going for the long duration, and we are told that magic is also employed.

These Indians are good runners. When they were asked to consider running in the 1932 Olympic marathon they regarded it as far too short, even for the women, who run over about sixty miles. Bruce ran about twenty kilometres with one of their best runners, called Ramon, a small thin man who seemed to be in his mid-forties. As a serious professional he would not race unless Bruce put up a substantial wager, but he ran 20k effortlessly, without taking his hat off.

The Mexican runner Martinez, who was 4th in the Olympic 10000m when it was in Mexico City, used to run against the Tarahumaras, but he never managed to win.

Running has always been with us and one of the great fascinations is trying to discover just how good these runners were. In medieval times, country fairs would include races, just as Highland Games do today, but these would be over irregular distances with no time-keeping.

There is a record of a race over 82 km in Rheims in 1592, which was won in twelve hours, but the fact that it has been remembered suggests that it was an unusual event.

The first professional runners were the foot messengers employed by kings, nobles and governments. The Incas of Peru had a fast and reliable system of relay runners who carried messages for the Inca to and from all corners of his empire. There is a record of King Malcolm of Scotland organising a race to select King's Messengers. The messengers of the Mogul empire in India were said to run eighty to ninety miles a day and one of the messengers of the Turkish Sultan ran two hundred kilometres from Constantinople to Adrianople in less than twenty-four hours. The most outstanding of all was the Norwegian Ernst Mensen, who carried messages for the royal houses of Europe. Since the letters he carried were dated, the times are probably correct. This man ran from Paris (the Place Vendôme) to Moscow (the gate of the Kremlin) in 1832, covering the 1550 miles/2500km in 14 days and 5 hours, an average of 108 miles/175 km per day. This may seem hard to believe, but this particular run was a well-documented professional venture, publicised in advance, so there is no reason to doubt its accuracy.

In the last few years the Greek ultra-runner Jannis Kouros has produced performances on the same level, running over 1000 km round the track in six days and running over 170 miles within twenty-four hours. Mensen then went on to run from Constantinople to Calcutta and back, a distance of 5187 miles/8300 km, in 59 days of running, an average of 88 miles a day. If this is true, Mensen was the greatest ultra-distance runner who ever lived. Sadly, he died of dysentery in 1843, at the age 47, while attempting to run to the source of the Nile

In the seventeenth and eighteenth centuries, the records we have are mostly of these professional runners, running races for a wager or a purse, rather like prize fighters. Towards the end of the eighteenth century, as roads became better and watches more accurate, the emphasis shifted. Both amateur and professional runners attempted standard distances. Foster Powell, who walked from London to York and back, set a 100-mile record of 21 hr 20 in 1762. The famous Captain Barclay Allardyce covered 1000 miles in 1000 hours, doing a mile every hour over a measured course on Newmarket Heath in 1809. One mile an hour does not sound like a lot, but think of never getting more than an hour's sleep at a time, for six weeks!

Incidentally, although Captain Barclay would have called himself a gentleman, his winnings were £16,000, in an age when £1 a week was a normal wage, so in present-day terms it was like winning millions.

These pedestrian feats aroused tremendous public interest and also attracted the gambling elements who were so much in evidence at prize-fights and cock-fighting. In 1815 a man called George Wilson set out to run a 1000 miles in 20 days on Blackheath Common, where today's London Marathon starts. Enormous crowds turned out, to watch and to gamble. Tents were set up around the course, providing food, drink and entertainment, which increased the crowding. There were pipers, fire-eaters, jugglers and even an elephant. Eventually, things got completely out of hand, the crowds flooded onto the course and George Wilson had to employ men with whips and staves to keep it clear. He had reached 751 miles and was on schedule to reach his target when the law intervened. The magistrates closed down the whole show and charged the unfortunate Wilson with causing a breach of the peace.

It was around this time that women and girls made their appearance as pedestrians. In 1836 Mary Firth ran 30 miles a day for 20 days and the following year Esther Crozier set out to emulate George Wilson by running 50 miles a day for 20 days. However she gave it up after 7 days, 'over some dispute'. In 1833 a 70-year-old woman made an attempt to run 96 miles in 24 hours in Paisley, Scotland. After 10 hours, when she had covered 45 miles, she suffered the same fate as George Wilson, because the crowd of spectators had become so loud and unruly as to constitute a threat to law and order. The most successful of these women was Mary McMullen, an Irishwoman whose sons were itinerant pedestrians. She was in her 60s in 1826–27 when she took part in a series of races, running distances of up to 90 miles. At the other end of the age spectrum, a girl called Emma Matilda Freeman competed in four events in nine weeks, at the age of 8, over distances of 30 to 40 miles.

It must be remembered that this was an era of great poverty and hardship in Britain. The feats of these pedestrians, like those of some African runners today, were driven by extreme need. Running as a mass sport really only came in with more widespread education and increasing leisure in the mid-19th century. The earliest known athletic club in Britain was the Necton Guild, founded in 1817, but the oldest surviving club, Exeter College, Oxford, was founded in 1850 and the first athletics club in London dates from 1864. The public schools introduced running as part of their sporting system, and Rugby School claims the honour of establishing the first cross-country event, the Crick Run, which has been held annually since 1837.

For a while, the amateur and professional branches of the sport flourished side by side, rather as boxing does today, with a growing number of local amateur clubs and a small number of professional individuals, some of whom performed to a very high standard. William Howitt was the first man to run 11 miles in the hour in 1845, on the road, and seven years later he achieved the same on a grass track. His performances were soon eclipsed by the the American runner Louis 'Deerfoot' Bennet, who toured Britain and Ireland in the 1860s. Deerfoot was an American Indian, and sometimes ran in native costume, with a feather in his head-band, which greatly increased his publicity value. His races were usually challenge events against local heroes, and sometimes record attempts against the clock. In April 1863, at the Brompton track., he set a world best for the one hour run of 11 miles 790yds/18.589km, going through 10 miles in 51mins 26. This was far ahead of anything the amateur runners of the time were doing, and the one hour record lasted for forty years, until Alfred Shrubb ran 18.742km in 1904.

Louis 'Deerfoot' Bennet

The ten mile mark was narrowly beaten by Walter George in 1884. He was the greatest runner of the late nineteenth century and the man who brought the amateur sport up to the level of the old pros. He lived from 1858 to 1943, and while living through the greatest social changes ever seen, he made his mark in his own field.

By 1880, when the Amateur Athletic Association was formed, there was an established system of inter-club matches, cross-country in the winter and track and field in the summer, with national championships in both branches of the sport. The first American Championships were held in 1876. Walter George won the AAA One Mile and Four Miles titles in 1880 and two years later won the cross-country, the One Mile, Four Miles and Ten miles. In 1884, the year he broke the ten-mile record, he again won all four distance running titles, setting world amateur records for the one mile (4:18.04) and four miles (20:12). With no worlds left to conquer, he turned professional and pitted himself against William Cummings, the Scot who held the professional record with 4 mins 16. In 1886 they had an epic battle, before a huge crowd. George, who had reputedly run under 4mins 10 for a time-trial mile, went out fast, with a first lap of 58.5 seconds. He went through the half-mile in just under 2:02, by which time he had broken the gap, and carried on to finish in 4:12.75 secs. This record stood until 1915, and it was not until 1931 that the 4:10 mark was offically broken. George went on to coach a number of British runners, and it was his training method which inspired Gosta

Holmer, the Swedish coach, to devise the Fartlek system.

The new form of the sport was ostentatiously amateur, distancing itself from the despised professionalism of the earlier pedestrians. In less sophisticated parts of the country, money continued to be awarded. In Scotland, Ireland and the Lake District, professional races and sports meetings continued to flourish well into the 20th Century, right up to the time when the so-called amateurs were officially allowed to be paid for winning races.

In the new world of amateur running, the oldest long distance race is the "Round the Bay" race at Lake Ontario, Canada, which was first held on Christmas Day 1894. It thus preceded by less than two years the first Olympic Marathon, which triggered off the first 'marathon boom'.

The first Modern Olympic Games in Athens in 1896 did not attract much attention from the world's Press. Only 59 athletes took part in the 10 track and field events, and sixteen of these (twelve of them Greek) ran in the marathon Since this is a history of running rather than of the Olympic movement, we shall confine ourselves to the things we are interested in.

The 800m and 1500m races were won by the lone Australian, Edwin Flack, in 2:11 and 4:33 secs respectively. The Marathon, as we all know, was won by Spyros or Spiridon Louis. His time was a mere 2 hr 58 for the approximate 25 miles/40km, but it is not generally realised that Louis, like all the Greek runners, had had to run a qualifying race shortly before the Games. His endurance was undoubtedly due to the fact that he had been jogging 14 kilometres twice a day alongside his mule, delivering water to Athens from his native village.

The Olympic Marathon was a new event for the sport, put in specially to signify Greece's great contribution to Western civilization, and it was this event which captured public imagination. The distance is just too far for most people, even well-trained for fifteen to twenty miles of fast running. Being quite different in its demands, it requires different abilities, and cannot be dominated by the typical big-boned long-striding middle-distance runner. It is an event in which a well-trained tortoise can beat an over-confident hare. Furthermore, it is so damned hard that just finishing a marathon race puts you into a different category from other human beings. A number of Marathons were staged later in 1896 and in 1897, but the only one which has survived to the present day is the Boston Marathon, which has become the repository of so much legend and mystique.

The continuity of the Boston Marathon has been hugely significant in developing the world-wide culture of long-distance running. From the start it has been a people's event, accessible to anyone who was prepared to do the work, and although the stars of Boston are now rich professional athletes, there is still nothing to stop a talented young American or Canadian from joining them. A similar position was held in England by the Polytechnic Marathon, which for many years followed the same course as the 1908 Olympic Marathon, from

Windsor Castle to the outskirts of London. Later, in 1921, the Comrades Marathon (54 miles) began, which has filled a similar role in South Africa.

The Windsor to London course occupies its own place in history. In the 1908 Olympic marathon the first person to cross the line was the little Italian, Dorando Pietri. He passed the previous leader just before he entered the stadium, only to collapse on the track. Doctors rushed to revive him and he got up and tottered to the line. He was almost carried over the line and immediately taken away for resuscitation. The second man JJ Hayes of America, finished without assistance and the Americans rightly put in a protest. After a long delay, Hayes was given the gold medal, but Pietri was given a gold cup by Queen Alexandra, and the whole episode renewed interest in the marathon as the ultimate in physical challenge. It was at this time that the distance became fixed as 26 miles 385 yards (42.195km). The course was planned as 26 miles, starting outside Windsor Castle and finishing on the track at the White City Stadium in Shepherd's Bush, London. However, at the Queen's request, the start was moved back into the castle grounds, so that the royal children could watch it from their apartments.

Paavo Nurmi

The Nurmi era

The distance running world has in the past had a strong Anglo-Saxon bias to it, but in the early part of the 20th century it was the Scandinavians, notably the Finns, who showed the way. This small country, struggling for independence from Russia, produced individuals with great fortitude, or *sisu*, as they called it. The first in a line of great athletes were the Kohlemainen brothers, Hannes and Willi. In the 1912 Olympics Hannes Kohlemainen won the 5000m, the 10000m and the cross-country. In the 5000metres he had a tremendous battle with the Frenchman, Jean Bouin. No one had run the distance in under 15 minutes before, but here both men ran 14:36 – superhuman. Would people then have believed that it would ever come down to under 14 minutes, let alone 13 minutes? (Haile Gebreselassie holds the 5000m record at the moment, with 12:39.) The onset of World War I prevented the holding of the 1916 Olympics, but when the Games resumed in Antwerp in 1920,

Hannes Kohlemainen won the marathon and Paavo Nurmi won the 10000m and the cross-country, as well as taking second in the 5000m. In the five Olympic Games held between the two World Wars, the Finns, with a little help from the Swedes, won almost all the medals in the 5000m, 10000m, cross-country, steeple-chase and marathon. On several occasions they had a clean sweep of the medals, prompting people to talk of 'special gifts' and 'genetic advantages', just as we do with the East Africans today.

The most outstanding of the Finns was Paavo Nurmi, who became the personification of distance running over more than a decade. He won four gold medals in the 1924 Games (1500m, 3000m team race, 5000m and cross-country.), a gold and two silvers in the 1928 Games, and would undoubtedly have won the 1932 marathon had he not been declared a professional a few days before.

What was remarkable about Nurmi was the fact that he trained all the year round – something never done before – and he seemed to run primarily for his own satisfaction. He made a science of running at level-pace, holding a stop-watch in his hand as he did so. He proved once and for all that level-pace running is the most efficient way.

Arthur Newton after winning the 1924 Comrades Marathon – but the horse beat him!

The Newton story

At the same time that Nurmi was dominating the tracks, a vastly different figure was making history in the world of road running.

Arthur Newton, born in England in 1883, emigrated to South Africa at the age of 18 and eventually became a farmer in what was then Southern Natal. After serving in World War One he returned to farming, but suffered a series of mishaps. In order to obtain some publicity for the farmer's cause he decided to become a runner. In his own words: "Winning a widely-advertised annual race would, I thought, enable me to turn a spotlight on to this cause which would in turn bring about legislation to rectify matters." He succeeded in his aim, but Arthur Newton's name lives on long after the cause of the tobacco farmer has been forgotten.

The race he was aiming at was the Comrades Marathon, which had been started earlier that year. The course for the Comrades runs from Durban to Pietermaritzburg, or vice versa, a distance of 88 km (54 miles), or more than twice the standard marathon. The 'up' and 'down' courses are run in alternate years; the difference in altitude is about 3000 ft (900m), but the ups and downs on the course make it even tougher. For many distance runners, particularly in South Africa, the Comrades is the ultimate challenge and the Olympic marathon distance a mere dash.

On January 1st 1922, Arthur Newton, aged 38, started his training for the Comrades' Marathon, which was due to take place on May 24th. He set out to run two miles, which he managed with difficulty. The next day he was very stiff and could not run for two days, but he persevered and got up to running ten miles after five weeks of training. After a disastrous experience in his first time trial, he decided to run purely for distance, without worrying about the pace. In his first Comrades he started slowly, two hundred yards behind the next man after a mile, but came through to win by half an hour, in a time of 8 hr 40.

Now here comes the curious thing. Newton was 38, and he had achieved his goal of gaining publicity on four months of hard training. Most people would have given up there, but for Newton it was just the beginning. He was hooked on running, and he was learning about himself. He was also laying down the basic principles of modern distance running. In the year before the next Comrades'race he covered overed 5000 miles (8000 km) in running and 1500 miles (2400km) in walking. He was running a regular 100 miles a week, with one day's rest.

When he came to the 1923 Comrades he ran the 'down' course in 6 hr 56 mins, beating the time of the first race by over two hours and finishing 52 minutes ahead of the next man. He went on to win it five times in a row and he lowered the course record to 6 hr 14 mins. Perhaps more significantly, he came to England and broke the record for the well-established London to Brighton run by 65 minutes. In 1927 he set new world best times for all distances from 30 to 100 miles, improving the latter record from 16 hr 7 mins to 14 hr 43.

In 1928 he took part in the first ever Trans-Continental Race from Los Angeles to New York. He had to retire from it through injury, as he did in 1929 when it was run in the reverse direction, but he ran a number of professional races in Canada and the USA, and in 1931, at the age of 47, he attempted the world 24-hour record. The run took place on a square indoor track, thirteen laps to the mile, and Newton covered 152 miles, 540 yds (245.1 km), which stood as a world record until 1953.

Newton's last world record was set when he was 51. Running on the Bath Road, (the A4) from Box to Hyde Park Corner, he improved on his own best time for 100 miles, reducing it to 14 hr 6. His comment was: "I had completely failed to put up a reasonable time on the course and I was too old to think of continuing for another year or two."

For the remainder of his life, until his death at the age of 75, Newton wrote books on running and continued to support the efforts of those who were trying to beat his records. Compared to those who came before him, Newton was revolutionary in stating the need to run all the year round and to make 20 mile runs a regular part of training for long-distance athletes.

Between the wars

During this inter-war period the USA was always the dominant nation in Olympic track and field, but the British did well on the track. Albert Hill did the 800/1500m double in 1920 and Douglas Lowe won the Olympic 800m in 1924 (the year that Eric Liddell won the 400m and Harold Abrahams the 100m) and retained his title with a world-record performance in 1928. In the marathon, Britain had consecutive silver medals in 1932 and 1936, and this event continued to throw up dramatic events and interesting individuals. The Algerian El Ouafi won for France in 1928 and 1936 saw the Korean Kitei Son winning for Japan – and running the first official sub 2 hr 30 marathon in the Olympic Games.

After World War II

When the world got back to normal after World War II, the Olympics were held in London, and they were televised. This, in a very small way, was the start of a new era in sport, through which athletes of all disciplines have been brought to the public. Sportsmen and women have become great heroes in the past, first through the papers and then the newsreels, but the TV screen, with its replays, its closeups, its live action, in-your-face, round-the-clock capacity, has enabled us to identify far more closely with those heroes.

However, it was not until the 1960s that televised sport had a really big impact on public consciousness, and it was some decades after that before the money from TV started to affect the competitive pattern of running.

The structure of the sport in the Western world continued much as it had in the 1930s, on a mainly amateur basis. In England, under the umbrella of the Amateur Athletic Association there were hundreds of amateur clubs. It was mainly a working-class sport, with a leaven of university runners. Business Houses such as Shell and Lloyds Bank maintained sports grounds and organised teams and institutions such as the Police, the Railways and the Armed Forces had a similar paternalistic approach to sport. In the United States, track and field was almost entirely college-based, and only a few traditional road races, like the Boston Marathon, provided competitive opportunities for distance runners.

Women's distance running

Before WWII, athletics for women was confined to a small number of clubs, and long distance running for women was almost unknown. In 1928, the 800m for women was included for the first time (and won in a world record 2:16.8 secs), but because several of the runners finished in a distressed state, the anti-feminist lobby in the IAAF persuaded that body to ban races longer than 200m. The way back was a long one. The 800m was introduced into the European Championships in 1954 and came back into the Olympics in 1960. In 1954, the year that Roger Bannister broke the four-minute mile, Diane Leather of London Olympiades became the first woman to break the five-minute mile barrier. The 1500m for women came in in 1972, but there were no longer events for women in the Olympic programme until the Los Angeles Games of 1984. The strong women's movement in America had by then forced the IOC and IAAF to include the marathon and the 3000m in the regular programme. The 10000m was added to the programme for the 1988 games and the 5000m replaced the 3000m in 1996. At the time of writing the Steeplechase and the Decathlon are still experimental events for women, but it will not be long before the two sexes follow exactly the same track and field programme.

Apart from the ocasional lone entry in a men's race, the history of women's marathon running really begins with the Australian runner Adrianne Beames, who ran 2 hr 46:30 in 1971. With the increase in 'mass participation' events, the record came down rapidly; Grete Waitz, nine times winner of the women's section of theNew York Marathon, improved it several times and in 1981 Allison Roe, of New Zealand, won the New York Marathon in 2 hr 25:29. In the 1983 Boston Marathon, Joan Benoit brought it down to 2 hr 22:43. She went on to become the first Olympic Marathon champion in Los Angeles the following year and, 18 years after her world best, we have just had the first sub-2 hr 20 from a woman.

The Zatopek era

Meanwhile, back in the Fifties, the distance running world was dominated by some remarkable Europeans. The greatest of these was Emil Zatopek, of Czechoslovakia. In 1952, at the Helsinki Olympics, he won the 5000 metres, the 10000m and the Marathon, a unique feat. It is only right that Zatopek should occupy this place in Olympic history, because he was a truly remarkable man, with an unequalled ability to absorb training. Moreover, he ran for the best possible reasons – because he loved running and because wanted to be as good as

Emil Zatopek

he possibly could be. His training sessions remain legendary – in 1948/49 he was running well over 200 km (125 miles) a week, with interval sessions of up to 60 x 400m on the track, and 40 x 400m on a regular basis. On top of all this he remained a friendly and unassuming man, a lifelong ambassador for his sport.

Zatopek transformed our ideas of what could be achieved in training and racing. Hot on his heels, succeeding him as European 5000m champion, came the tough Ukrainian, Vladimir Kuts, who in a series of dramatic races brought the world record for that event down from Zatopek's 13:57 in 1954 to 13:35 in 1957. This was only forty-odd years after Kohlemainen and Jean Bouin had broken through the 15-minute barrier.

It was during the Cold War era that athletes from the Communist bloc produced some remarkable performances. They were full-timers, amateurs in name only, because most of them were employed by the Army or the Police and given as much time as they wanted for training. Combined with the use of drugs, which in the case of East Germany has been shown to be a well-documented fact, they came to dominate women's athletics, but strangely enough they never had a huge impact on the world of distance running. Kuts and Zatopek were one-off individuals, and the men who came after them, though good, were unable to dominate.

A few British and Australian athletes survived as full-time runners, benefiting from the 'shamateur' system which operated on the Scandinavian circuit. Running has always been a popular sport in Scandinavia, so appearance money and prize money, sometimes disguised as expenses, sometimes handed over in the traditional brown envelope, have been tolerated for a long time. Paavo Nurmi was kicked out of the sport in 1932 for allegedly receiving illegal payments, but in the Fifties and Sixties it was commonly accepted. After Derek Ibbotson broke the world record for the mile in 1957, he embarked on a prolonged tour of Scandinavia, on the proceeds of which he built a house which he named "Myleta".

The next force to appear on the distance scene was that of the Hungarians under the coach Mihaly Igloi. Three of his runners were holders of the world record at 1500m, another broke the record for the 3000m steeplechase and the best of them, Sandor Iharos, broke the world records for 5000m and 10000m.

Unfortunately for them the Hungarian Revolution of 1956 came just before the Melbourne Olympics and Vladimir Kuts was able to complete a double in 5000 and 10000.

BRUCE: "Readers may be able to detect that the last fifty years are being covered in much more detail than the previous two thousand. From the 'Zatopek Olympics' of 1952 to the present day I have been a close student of the distance running scene, first as a spectator, then as a competitor, a coach and a journalist. It will not surprise them to learn that I consider the days of my youth to have been a 'golden era' in track running. There was a constant battle between athletes from different economic systems – the college-based Americans, the 'professional' East Europeans and the amateurs and shamateurs of Britain, Australia and New Zealand."

Although Britain derived a lot of kudos from Roger Bannister's first four-minute mile in 1954, and the records of Gordon Pirie, Derek Ibbotson and Chris Chataway, it was the runners from down under who brought new methods into the sport and set new standards.

The classic European training method of the 1950s was interval training. The interval system had been developed by the German physiologist, Waldemar Gerschler, in the thirties, with remarkable effects. The Austrian coach, Franz Stampfl, produced a book, *Stampfl on Running*, which became the Bible of most serious athletes. Here is a sample of the Three Miles (5000m) training schedule for April. All British tracks were then 440 yards, which is 402m.

All sessions start with 20 mins warm-up and 5 mins rest and are followed by a warm-down jog

Monday	20 x 440 yds in 69 secs (2½–3 mins recovery lap)
Tuesday	5 x 3 laps in 3:27, 10 mins rest between
Wednesday	15 x 440 yds in 65 secs (lap jog recovery)
Thursday	3 x 5 laps in 5:50, 10 mins rest between
Friday	4 miles run, on the track, 20 mins
Saturday	one hour easy Fartlek
Sunday	rest

You can follow this schedule, as Bruce did, and it will make you a lot fitter, but it is very boring and on a synthetic track it would soon lead to injury.

In the late fifties and the early Sixties, two remarkable coaches were developing their own training methods. Percy Cerrutty, in Australia, was a great believer in 'natural' living. He hated cities, roads, tracks, junk food and women in

Peter Snell – triple Olympic champion

training camps. He believed in strength training and in running hard in natural surroundings. He built a house out in the sand dunes at Portsea, near Melbourne, which became the base of a great group of athletes. The most notable of these was Herb Elliott, who went through his career undefeated at one mile or 1500m, and broke the world record while winning the 1500m at the Rome Olympics, at the age of twenty-two. A typical day at the Portsea training camp is described by Alan Trengove in his biography of Elliott (*The Golden Mile*, pub. Cassell, 1961)

7.00 am	5 miles run and a dip in the ocean
8.00 am	breakfast of rolled oats, wheat germ, walnuts and banana
12.00 am	main training session and another swim
2.00 pm	lunch of fish and fresh fruit
4.00 pm	weightlifting
5.00 pm	5–10 mile run on beach and dirt roads
7.00 pm	supper and general discussion
11.00 pm	lights out

This schedule of well over twenty miles a day is very similar to the routine followed in Kenyan training camps today, with the addition of swimming, weightlifting and better food – but without the 2000m altitude.

Meanwhile, in New Zealand, Arthur Lydiard was developing his own ideas and coaching the lads in his Auckland neighbourhood. Does the coach make the athlete or the athlete make the coach? It must be more than coincidental that this small group of athletes included two of the greatest runners of their era, Murray Halberg and Peter Snell, who between them broke the world records for the half mile, mile, two miles and three miles and won Olympic gold medals at 800m, 1500m and 5000m.

Like Cerutty, Lydiard built his system out of his own experiences as a successful marathon runner, based on self-reliance and a high mileage, mostly off the track. Lydiard was by no means the first coach to have his athletes running 100 miles a week – Zatopek had far exceeded that, but he was the first to formulate this as the basis of training from 1500m upwards. He can also claim some credit for starting the 'jogging boom', because of the influence he had on Bill Bowerman.

Ron Clarke – barrier breaker

Lydiard and Cerutty enjoyed their successes in the Olympics of 1960 and 1964, as well as in the Commonwealth Games of '58, and '62, only to be eclipsed by the performances of another Australian, Ron Clarke. Clarke is famous for setting world records but never winning a gold medal in a major games. After narrowly beating the world 10000m record in 1964, with 28:15, he smashed through the 28-minute barrier the following year, with an amazing 27:39, and also took the 5000m record way below the 13.30 mark, with 13:16.

These were times which were believed impossible, yet not only did athletes appear who could stay with Clarke and outsprint him, some of them went on to improve on his records.

Clarke was unlucky in that the peak of his career coinided with two other events – the first ever 'altitude Olympics' and the emergence of the African runners.

The altitude factor

In 1968 the Games were held in Mexico City, at an altitude of 2400m/7500ft. This made life easier for the explosive events, as we saw with Bob Beamon's amazing long jump world record, but much more difficult for distance runners, who had to cope with the shortage of oxygen. Those who coped best were those who were either born at high altitude or had spent a lot of time there.

Kip Keino – leader of the Kenyan breakthrough, the double Olympic gold medallist

The athletes from East Africa had shown signs of talent earlier, with Abebe Bikila winning the Olympic marathon in 1960 and '64 and the Kenyans Keino and Temu winning gold medals in the Commonwealth Games, but here they emerged as Olympic champions. Keino won the 1500m and placed second in the 5000m; Temu won the 10000m and got a bronze in the 5000m, while the marathon was won by the Ethiopian Mamo Wolde, who had won the silver medal in the 10000m.

From that time on, the African domination of distance running has become more and more established. The other effect of the Mexico Games was to demonstrate the benefits of training at altitude. The Soviet Union athletes were using altitude training in the 1960s, and since the Mexico Games altitude camps have been developed all over the world, some purpose-built and well-equipped, like the French centre at Font Romeu, in the Pyrenees, or the Swiss centre at Davos, others merely places where athletes live and train, like Boulder, Colorado or Eldoret and Nyahururu in Kenya.

Money matters

During the 1970s the effects of television brought more and more money into sport, and 'shamateurism' became more prevalent in European and America. The world's biggest track and field meetings, such as those in Monte Carlo, Helsinki, Oslo and Rome, were receiving huge television and sponsorship fees and were competing amongst one another in offering appearance fees to athletes. Eventually the governing body of the sport, the International Amateur Athletic Federation, was forced into tolerance of a *de facto* professionalism, and they allowed money to be paid into athletes' trust funds for future use. Soon it was allowed to draw expenses from these funds, and by the early eighties, athletes were allowed to receive cash 'subventions', whilst still remaining officially

Seb Coe – the only man to retain the Olympic 1500m title

amateurs. Now we have reached a point where, although the Olympics remain technically amateur, medal-winners are paid large sums by their countries and their sponsors, and the IAAF world championship events carry tens of thousands of dollars in prize money.

Some of the first athletes to benefit from the open payment of money for running were the great British trio of middle distance runners, Seb Coe, Steve Ovett and Steve Cram.

In the 1980 Olympics Ovett won the 800m and Coe the 1500m, and their rivalry was fought out on the tracks of the world for the next four years. In 1981 Ovett and Coe both broke the world records for 1500m and the Mile, and Coe set a world record for the 800m which stood for 18 years. In the Los Angeles Games Coe retained his 1500m title, while the silver medal was won by Cram, the 1983 World Champion, who later went on to set a world record of 3:46 secs for the Mile.

The rise of the Africans

The Coe-Ovett era was a golden one for British athletics, and the press often lament its passing, but in fact the decline is not so much a British one as a Western one. Just as the Finns and Swedes lost their pre-eminence as the sport became more widespread, so the vast increase in the number of participating countries has led to the money and the medals being more widely shared. There are now more than 200 countries in the IAAF, and in the Sydney Olympics more than fifty countries won at least one medal. Distance running is a poor man's sport, and nowhere are people poorer than in Africa. Once the people of East Africa discovered that running offered a way of making a good living, more and more of them started competing overseas. The Ethiopians and the Kenyans dominate the cross-country, the steeplechase, the marathon and the longer track distances. In the late Seventies the Kenyan Henry Rono set world records for the 5000m, the 10000m and the Steeplechase, but in the next decade these were eclipsed not only by his fellow countrymen such as Moses Kiptanui and Daniel Komen but also by the North Africans. The Algerian Said Aouita broke the records for 1500m and 5000m; he was followed by Noureddine Morceli, and in the Nineties the Moroccans started to come through, led by Skah and Hissou. The Moroccan El Guerrouj is the current holder of the 1500m and Mile records; Kenyans hold the records for the 3000m, the Steeplechase and the 800m, and the records for the two longer track races are held by the Ethiopian Haile Gebreselassie, at 12:39 and 26:22 respectively. We have come a long way since the days of Kohlemainen.

The African domination has not been so marked in women's events, because for cultural reasons many women have not in the past been given a chance to compete. Those who have done so, though, have come to lead the world. Derarta Tulu of Ethiopia is Olympic champion at the 10000metres and a winner of the London Marathon, and her compatriots Gete Wami and Fatuma Roba have also held world and Olympic titles in cross-country, 10000m and marathon. The leading women in the latter event are Kenyan – Tecla Loroupe, Joyce Chepchumba and Catherine Ndereba, but they are closely challenged by runners from Japan, China, Mexico and Romania as well as by the Ethiopians.

The jogging boom

One of the trends pushing the sport towards professionalism has been the growth of road racing. Throughout the twentieth century road racing and road relay racing were a regular part of the club athlete's programme, but until about 1970 the sport was mainly confined to young men, and the race distances rarely exceeded ten miles, but then things started to change. It was the start of the 'jogging boom'.

The spread of running in the seventies was due to an increase in leisure, combined with an increasing awareness of the relationship between exercise and health. One cannot pick on a single cause – some say it was Frank Shorter's victory in the 1972 Olympic Marathon which captured the American public's imagination, and Bruce likes to think that his run from Los Angeles to New York had something to do with it (Forrest Gump got the credit for it). However, the origins start earlier than that. In 1962 the University of Oregon coach Bill Bowerman took his team on a tour of New Zealand. He was very impressed by the high level of vitality he saw among the New Zealanders, particularly amongst the over-30s.

The coach Arthur Lydiard had started to form jogging groups, where people of all ages could combine companionship with easy running. Bowerman, then aged fifty, joined in with a group of 200 men women and children.

"After half a mile, he was alone again. Only a 76-year-old man was nearby. As the two jogged, the old gentleman's presence became painful to an already bruised ego; the old fellow was holding himself back, waiting for Bowerman." His experiences in New Zealand impressed Bowerman greatly, and when he returned home he started to talk to people about it, and to talk to the press. In America sport had always been considered the concern of high schools, colleges and professional athletes – it was not something for the average man, who was supposed to have his mind on more gainful occupations. When this attracted public interest and people started asking him about jogging, he decided to conduct a controlled programme of running for adults, with the help of a cardiologist who was interested in preventing heart disease. This in turn led to the publication of *Jogging – A Physical Fitness Programme For All Ages*, written by Bill Bowerman and Dr WE Harris and published in 1967 by Grosset and Dunlap, from which the above quotation is taken. This book, along with Dr. Kenneth Cooper's book on *Aerobics*, became the handbook of the fitness enthusiasts.

On the other side of the continent, another enthusiast was trying to establish the New York Marathon. Fred Lebow, who sadly died of cancer only a few years ago, organised the first New York Marathon in 1970, funding it out of his own pocket. The first race was run in Central Park; it attracted 55 runners and his total budget was a thousand dollars; by its sixth year, the numbers were into four figures and the advertisers and sponsors were beginning to take notice. In 1976 the decision was taken to take the race through all the five boroughs of New York City. Over two thousand people ran, Bill Rodgers and Frank Shorter placed first and second and the race went on to become the national event it is today, with over thirty thousand runners and a worldwide TV audience of 100 million.

Some people ascribe the jogging boom to Jim Fixx, whose book

The Complete Book of Running appeared in 1977 and was a runaway success. Fixx's first achievement, however, was not in starting the boom but in recognising it. As he said himself in 1976, when he was writing outlines for potential publishers: "the jogging fad of five or six years ago has finally blossomed into a major boom". His second achievement was in writing a book which was so thorough, so readable and so well presented that it became a major best-seller. This led directly to his third achievement, which really did have an effect on the sport. By selling over a million copies of his book in hardback. Jim Fixx trumpeted a signal to the marketing men of America that running was an important part of American life. The magazine sales soared, advertisers flooded in, new road races attracted sponsors and the sales of sportswear and running shoes climbed steeply. One of the beneficiaries of this, incidentally, was Bill Bowerman, who was one of the founders of the running shoe company Nike.

Although Lydiard, Bowerman and Fixx will always retain their places in the history of our sport, the running boom would probably have happened without them. They were the men preaching the message at a time when society was ready to listen.

Marathon fever

In the first few years, the running boom was a marathon boom. The first London Marathon was held in 1981, and by 1985 there were 131 marathons in the United Kingdom. Since then the number of marathons in Britain has dropped to around forty a year, but the appeal of the big-city marathons remains as big as ever. London, New York and Boston cope with fields of around 30,000, but the number of applications is often double that. Similar mass-participation take place in all the big European capitals – Berlin, Paris, Stockholm and Budapest – and some of the half marathon races are even bigger, for example the City-to-Surf run in Sydney, Australia, the Great North Run in Newcastle (over 40,000) and the Stramilano in Milan, which claims to have 50,000 runners. The biggest race so far was the one held to mark the opening of the new bridge from Denmark to Sweden, which is said to have had 70,000 runners.

Public interest and television coverage go hand-in-hand. All the big marathons are now big TV events as well, which means that large sums are paid in prize money and appearance money to attract. the best athletes. Unfortunately this has tempted a number of runners to use drugs to improve their performance, notably EPO (erythropoietin) which has the effect of increasing the number of red blood cells. The men's world record, which stood at 2 hr 6:50 seconds for many years, was certainly due for revision, and is currently standing at 2 hr 5:44 secs, held by Khalid Kannouchi of Morocco, but the large numbers of runners going below 2 hr 7 leads us to suspect that not all of these performances are genuine.

The diversity of running

The last twenty years have seen an escalation of the number of running activities, and, as in the world of music, we see the emergence of diversity. The IAAF now have world cross-country, world half marathon and world road relay championships every year, as well as biennial world indoor and world outdoor athletics championships, mountain running championships and 100kilometres championships – but these are all at the elite level.

As a runner you may be involved in road, track or cross-country racing, in fell racing, orienteering, hashing, duathlon (run, bike, run), triathlon (swim, bike, run), modern pentathlon (ride, swim, fence, shoot and run) mountain running, trail running, ultra-running or adventure running.

The last four tend to overlap. Mountain running usually entails a course of 5–15 miles (8–24 km), sometimes from the bottom of the mountain to the top, sometimes up and back to the starting point, like the Ben Nevis race, sometimes starting from one town, over the mountain to another town. Trail running is a relatively new branch of the sport. Courses are multi-terrain, but not necessarily hilly, in the range of 5–12 miles (8–20 km). The term 'Ultra-running' usually means 'anything longer than a standard marathon', but includes off-road events of 20 miles or longer.

Adventure racing usually involves events outside the United Kingdom, and may involve things other than running. The most famous or infamous is probably the 'Marathon des Sables', which is a French-organised seven-day event, covering up to 150 miles (240 km) carrying your own food, but there are many others which involve paddling canoes, mountain biking and even abseiling down cliffs as well as a lot of running. Since they are all long-distance endurance events the older runner has a better chance of success than in shorter faster races.

The future of running

Everyone wants to know how long records can go on improving. Every generation has said: "they've gone about as far as they can go". When Bruce wrote his first book, in 1967, he predicted what the men's records would be in 1980. This was based on the rate of improvement seen over the previous twenty years. Table 2 below shows how the predictions compare with the actual world records in 1980 and 2000.

Table 2: Predicted and actual World records

Distance	1967 (actual)	1980 (predicted)	1980 (actual)	2000 (actual)
800m	1:44.3	1:44.7	1:42.3	1:41.1
1500m	3:33.1	3:28.0	3:32.0	3:26.0
5000m	13:16.6	12:57.0	13:08.4	12:39.3
10000m	27:39.0	26:48.0	27:22.5	26:22.7

Two things stand out – first, that the rate of improvement has been slower than expected and second that all the records for 2000 are considerably better than the predictions for 1980.

Records will go on getting better, but only very slowly. The men's 100m record has only improved by 0.16 since 1968.

The biggest factor is the increase in the numbers of people in the sport. Although most of the African nations now send athletes to major events, in the two largest nations on earth, China and India, few of the population are encouraged to run. In the highlands of Asia and South America there must be populations of people who are adapted to running at high altitudes, like the Ethiopians and Kenyans, but who have not yet been involved in competition.

We would predict that by 2020 the records will look like this:

Table 3: Predictions for 2020

Men

Distance	2020 (predicted)
800m	1:40.8
1500m	3:24.5
5000m	12:31
10000m	26:02

Women

Distance	2000 (actual)	2020 (predicted)
800m	1:53.3	1:51.9
1500m	3:50.4	3:48.5
5000m	14:28.1	14:20.0
10000m	29:31.8	29:30.0

In women's running one would expect that the rate of improvement of records would be faster, because distance running for women started much more recently and most of the events were not even being held thirty years ago. Against that, there is a strong suspicion that the existing records, all set by Eastern bloc athletes, were set with the help of drugs, Experience has shown that what is achieved with drugs can eventually be achieved without them, but we would not expect the improvements to be huge.

The future for over-forties

In the sport as a whole we will see an even greater diversity of running-based sports being offered to an ever-widening range of age-groups. The division between competitive sport and 'fun-running' will become wider, with the latter forming the bulk of the events.

One can safely predict that we shall all get older, and as more top-class athletes get older and have the leisure to continue running, we shall find that over-40 records actually close the gap on the under-forties. Similarly, with greater participation (and better medical care) the older age-group records will improve even faster, so that there will no longer be any 'soft' records.

At the time of writing the centenarian records are mostly vacant, but hopefully some of those reading this book will be able to fill in the blanks!

Nigel Gates

age: **48** occupation: **special needs teacher**

Nigel Gates is the supreme competitor of his day, amongst British vets at least. A runner of top national level in his thirties, he has shown that a high level of fitness can be maintained more or less indefinitely if the will is there. He holds the British records for M40s and M45s at 10000m (30:25 for 10k on the track), as well as the British 5000m record for the M45 age group. He has won World veteran titles at 5000m and 10000m on the track and 10k on the road, as well as European titles for 3k indoors and for the 10k and the half marathon. Perhaps his best performances have been in cross-country, where he has won both the English vets title and the British title four times, as well as a World title.

"I was always keen on running, but I only started training when I was16, using books from the shcool library by Lydiard and Cerutty. At 18 I came 3rd in the English Schools cross-country and was also 3rd in the 1500m in the summer. In my 20s I wanted to be the next Brendan Foster; I ran for Britain at cross-country, road running and mountain running, but never made it to major games level, so I took off to Europe and ran up mountains. I found that I was almost unbeatable in short straight-up races. I think that the success factors here were related to the lack of pressure – no worries about speed and no chance of getting seriously famous.

"I love running because it connects me with nature and it is the only time I get to myself! It also mean travel and adventure. It is the only area of my life in which I seek to prove myself – I am too easy-going in everything else. I teach full time and so does my wife, so most of my running is door-to-door. On weekdays I run five miles cross-country at 6.45 am, plus 3–4 evening runs.

"On Saturday and Sunday mornings I train at 8.30 am, usually speedwork on the track or road on Saturday and a long run over the Seven Sisters on Sunday. This gives me the rest of the weekend to spend with my family.

"Since becoming forty I have found more important things in my life than running. I am much more focussed on what I want to achieve (wife Patricia's influence) and I peak well for crunch races. I am less concerned with speed and more concerned with fitness and health, so anaerobic work is minimized. If I had known more about the physiology when I was younger, and had had the confidence and attitude I have now, I think I could have made top level as a senior – but it isn't anything I regret because I am still fulfilling myself now."

CHAPTER FOUR

Clothing and equipment

"I'm not a jogger! I paid £100 for this tracksuit."

SHARMAN PATERSON, MARLBOROUGH RUNNING CLUB

If you are starting from scratch, your first few days of exercise will be walking, which can be done in everyday clothes. You will quickly find out that comfort is what matters most. Clothes should not be so tight as to chafe or restrict your movement, nor should they be so loose that they flap about. Shoes need to have rubber soles and be big enough for your foot to stretch out fully. They should be flat-heeled, with a bit of cushioning in the heel to absorb the shock of landing.

Before you reach the end of Stage One, though, you will need to buy yourself some proper running shoes. It is best to go to a specialist sports-shoe shop and try out the different makes. Some makes tend to be narrower, some wider, so you need to find the brand whose last matches your kind of feet. The heavier you are, the more cushioning you will need, but if you have too much cushioning your feet are further off the ground, which leads to instability.

Our advice is to go to a specialist shop, try on lots of brands and pick the one which feels right for you, regardless of the price – the most expensive is not necessarily the best. Remember that if you are buying a US size it will be one size larger than you take in British sizes. Although you can often get cheap shoes through mail order, we don't recommend it, unless you are familiar with the brand. Good fit is vital in running shoes, so you should try them on and jog up and down before buying. To start with, the most important thing for you will be comfort and protection, which means you should choose a fairly heavy well-padded shoe. As you become better adapted to regular running

Trudi Thomson – a GB international at 40. Note the gloves for cold-weather racing

you may prefer to run in something lighter, because the lighter the shoe, the easier it is to run. For Bruce, the most enjoyable running is in bare feet, either on the beach down in Devon or on well-kept playing fields. Running in bare feet enables you to use all the muscles in the foot in the way they were designed to work, so it makes your feet stronger, and it is faster – but there are drawbacks, which we needn't go into.

Specialist shoes

If you get into serious racing on the road, you should buy a light and flexible racing shoe – the nearest thing to bare feet. The difference between wearing heavy trainers and light racing shoes can be as much as ten seconds per mile – or a minute in a 10k race. The drawback is that the lighter the shoe, the less protection it gives and you run the risk of getting sore legs, so many people opt for a 'racer-trainer' which gives you some protection. The lightest racing shoe will be from about 6oz/170g to 10oz/280g, depending on the size of your foot; the trainer/racers will be in the range of 11–13oz/310–360g and the heavy training shoes will weigh as much as 16oz/450g. If you are running on the track, you can do this perfectly well in the racing flats you use on the road, but if you are going to run in sprints or middle-distance races you will probably need spikes. On normal synthetic tracks you must use spikes which are 5–6 mm long, but if you run on an old-fashioned grass or cinder track you will need 9 or 12 mm spikes. The advantage of the interchangeable spikes is that you can use them in the winter for cross-country running as well – here again the 9–12 mm length is suitable for most courses.

In recent years there has been an increase in multi-terrain races. These often start and finish with a mile or two of road before going off onto grassland or forest trails. You cannot use spikes because there is too much road, but if you use racing flats you may well slip about on muddy tracks. The answer is to buy rubber-studded shoes, but if you are buying them to race in they should not be too heavy. The best ones are those advertised for orienteering or fell racing, because they are usually lightweight and waterproof.

Marathon footwear

This is worth a paragraph to itself, because it is crazy to spend months training for the event and then ruin it through having the wrong shoes. Never wear new shoes for a marathon. Your racing shoes should be worn in but not worn out. If you feel you need new shoes, buy them a month before the race, wear them a few times in normal training and for your last two long runs. This will give you the chance to get the shoe/sock balance right. Ideally, marathon shoes should be half a size larger than the shoe you use for normal training, because your feet swell during a long race. If you buy a tight-fitting pair because they make your feet look smaller you will finish up – if you finish at all – with black toe-nails and blisters. You should wear a thick pair of socks with them in the short runs and a thin pair of socks for the marathon. To decrease the risk of getting blisters it is a good idea to put plenty of talcum powder inside the socks and inside the shoes before you race in them.

Clothing

It is possible to spend hundreds of pounds on expensive running gear. It won't make you run any faster. On the other hand, it is important to look good and feel good when running. If you go on running in the same shorts and t-shirt day after day without washing them you will find that it is unpopular as well as unhygienic. We recommend having four sets of everything, for the serious runner.

The things you will need are:

- **Shorts:** Can be as brief as modesty and climate permit, but many people find that the long cycling shorts, with Lycra in them, are very useful, because they prevent chafing.
- **T-shirts:** Not too tight. The right t-shirt can have tremendous status value.

- **Singlets:** Essential for hot weather running. Tight singlets are alright for short runs but uncomfortable in the long run.
- **Jogging bra:** Where appropriate. Can save a lot of unnecessary motion.
- **Long-sleeved t-shirts:** Very useful for cold weather running, because they keep the forearms warm.
- **Tights:** Strongly advised for both men and women when running in cold weather. The colder your muscles, the more likely you are to pull a muscle.
- **Anoraks:** otherwise called rain-tops, shells or wind-cheaters, should be shower-proof, with a hood.
- **Caps, hats, headbands and gloves:** These small items can make a huge difference to your comfort when running, because so much heat is lost from the head and the hands. The older you get, the more you need to keep your head warm. On the other hand there are times when you will need a headband to keep the sweat out of your eyes, or a peaked cap to protect you from glare. When running a cold-weather marathon it is well worth starting with a big t-shirt and an old woolly hat on top of everything. After a few miles, when you have generated enough heat, you can throw them away. (And, of course, if you need to collect some old t-shirts and woolly hats, just go to the start of the London Marathon on a cold day.)
- **Reflective clothing:** When running at night, few runners realise that although they can see the car, the car probably cannot see them until the last minute. Most running shoes have reflective heel tabs, but it is also essential to have reflective tape on the back of your clothing. The best things to get are bibs made of brightly coloured and reflective mesh, which make you visible both after dark and in dim light.
- **Dustbin liners:** In a really big race you may be hanging around for forty minutes at the start, having already handed in your tracksuit. A large waterproof plastic bag may not be the smartest thing to wear but if the weather is cold and wet it can save you a lot of discomfort.
- **Heart Monitor:** This is a useful, though not essential device, because it enables you to learn about yourself. As long as you use a 'chest strap'rather than a 'fingertip' model, even the cheapest monitor will enable you to find out about your resting heart rate, your 'comfortable', your 'threshold' and your maximum heart rate. By training at the right heart rate you can ensure that your running is doing you good and not doing you harm. The way to use them is described in the next chapter.

General clothing advice

When running, you get much hotter than you expect, and after running you get much colder than you expect. The experienced runner therefore goes for multiple layers of clothing rather than single thick garments.

For a race in average English conditions we would advise shorts, a singlet, in case it is warm, a t-shirt, which can be worn with or instead of the singlet if it is cold, a rain-top to protect you when warming-up and a fleecy sweater to put on after the race, as well as cap, gloves and tights to warm up in and tracksuit bottoms to keep you warm afterwards.

Accessories

- **First aid kit:** When going away to a big race or a training camp, we usually take the following:
  scissors, plasters, safety pins, roll of adhesive tape, antiseptic cream, foot powder, fungicidal cream, aspirin, Ibuprofen (tablets and ointment), diarrhoea tablets, indigestion tablets, massage oil, and a couple of bandages for strapping ankles. For hot-weather events we also take sun block, insect repellent and sting relief ointment.
- **Radios and Walkmen:** We don't recommend these, for two reasons. The first is that they make you deaf to traffic and therefore much more liable to have an accident, and the other is that you will run more effectively if you 'switch on' to what you are doing, rather than switiching off. However, they are a great help to those who find long runs boring.
- **Bum-bag:** Highly useful for carrying a spare sweater or shell in uncertain weather.
- **Armband:** The small armband with a Velcro strap and a pocket, as worn by skiers, is really useful, because you can carry your car keys, phone money, toilet paper etc., without worries.
- **Wristbands:** Only for the really pretentious.
- **Water-bottle:** Essential for the serious long-distance runner, because you can get dehydrated very easily. It is useful to have a small one which you can carry when running solo and a large one which you can get someone else to carry.

Pat Gallagher

age: **55** occupation: **administrator**

When you see Pat Gallagher run, you worry about her, because she pushes herself so hard. "Can this be wise?", one thinks, "surely she can't keep on doing this."

Pat started competing as a 13-year-old, and at 21 she ran for Wales in the World cross-country championships and then retired. Ten years later, following the death of her husband, Westbury Harriers persuaded her to return, and at 38 she was picked for Wales again, in the 800m. Her outstanding achievements, though, have all been as a veteran. She won her first of many World titles at the age of forty and she holds British veteran records for 800m and 1500m. In 2001 she raced little, because of injury, but still won both the 1500m and the 3000m in the European indoor championships, setting a W55 world record in the latter event. Like Nigel Gates, she has shown that hard training helps you to hold the years at bay. Her best 1500m time, set at the the age of 38, is 4:32 but she was able to record 4:49 for the distance as an over-fifty – a decline of less than 1 second per kilometre per year.

"I like the discipline of training – although I sometimes hate it – but it is such a good feeling when the hard work produces results.

"It is hard to fit in training with a full time job. I get up at 6 am – it's a wonderful time to train; with no one around you can plod along at your own pace. In the evening I train with the group and also help coach the youngsters. I do one speed session a week and one speed endurance session on the grass.

"I don't think my approach has changed, but I find myself more prone to injuries and health problems as I get older. I now try to be more aware of how my body feels. I hoped that this was going to be my year, turning 55, but I developed a Deep Vein Thrombosis. I am now training again – Never Give Up!"

CHAPTER FIVE

How to train properly

"Train first for distance, then for speed"

ARTHUR NEWTON

Basic principles

The simplest way of understanding training is to relate it to the distance you hope to run. If you want to race over 10 kilometres, you first have to build up your endurance to the point where you can cover at least 10 kilometres non-stop (walking is allowed) and then you have to work on your running speed. If you want to run the 10k in under fifty minutes, you have to start by running one kilometre in under five minutes. Getting the right mixture of endurance and speed training is dealt with in the schedules in later chapters.

Remember that the training process consists of Stimulus and Response. When you make an effort, the body will try to adjust so as to cope with that effort, and when it has adjusted you can increase the load a little bit more – either by increasing the distance or by increasing the speed. The human body is amazingly adaptable, but it needs time. The art of coaching lies in choosing the training which gives enough stimulus to have an effect, but not so much that it causes breakdown. If you just go on doing the same thing week after week you will not only get bored, you will cease to improve.

The most efficient way of operating is to vary the training, so that we are working on different aspects of fitness. The first principle, credited to Arthur Newton (see Chapter 3) is: "Train first for distance, then for speed". By walking and jogging, and later by continuous slow running, we strengthen our supporting system. The supporting muscles and ligaments, which keep our skeleton in position, will get stronger. The muscles will increase their fuel storage cpacity and in particular there will be a development of the tiny capillary blood vessels which surround the muscle fibes. This will greatly increase the ability of the blood to get oxygen into the working muscles.

Heavy weight-training may increase your muscle strength and the muscle fibes may get bigger, but it will have no effect on developing this important capillary bed, so all distance runners – even middle distance runners – need a foundation of long slow running.

Building up the total distance run each week will have other effects. It will burn up excess fat, reducing your body weight, and it will encourage the leg bones to lay down extra bone material, making the bones stronger and decreasing the risk of osteoporosis. However, this increase has to be gradual, because the shock of the repeated impact of foot on tarmac may cause damage to unprepared bones and joints. The human feet and legs are designed to run, but not to run on tarmac, so you should try to get off the road as much as possible, and if you do have to run on road a lot, make sure that you have good shoes.

"First and foremost, there is no substitute for properly structured training. Regardless of age, hard intensive work, with suitable recovery periods, is the only sure way of improving"

IAN VAUGHAN-ARBUCKLE

Increasing the speed

To run faster you have, for a start, to increase both your stride length and your rate of striking. This means that you have to drive more strongly and lift your knees higher. To maintain this extra speed needs a greater energy production and of course a greatly increased oxygen intake. You have to breathe harder and more deeply, and your heart has to pump harder to pick up more oxygen per minute. With training, all these capacities will improve. Most of us have enough lung capacity to take in the extra volume of air, but it is the effect of training on the cardiovascular system – the heart and the arteries – which influences our ability to run well.

The good runner has a large strong heart. This is partly due to his genetic background and partly to the training he has done. One thing is certain, that we can all improve our cardiovascular system by training. This can be shown easily by running round a certain course in a certain time and taking the pulse rate before and after. The duration of the timed run should be at least five minutes, but not more than ten minutes.

Let us say, for example, that you decide to run four times around the track – a mile – in seven minutes. For the unfit person this would be a hard effort and his pulse rate would probably go close to its maximum. However, for the fit person who can easily run a mile in under six minutes this pace will be quite easy and the pulse rate will not be as high. Over the years a number of changes have taken place in his body, which have made the seven-minute mile easy. Down in the muscles there has been a huge increase in the number of enzyme molecules which pick up the oxygen from the blood. There has also been a development of the capillary bed, so that the blood flows more easily through the muscles and an increase in the strength and capacity of the heart itself. The heart is a muscle – an exceptional one. It will get stronger with exercise, and the result of all these changes is that a seven-minute mile, which left you puffing and gasping with a pulse rate of a hundred and eighty beats per minutes, can soon be handled comfortably, with the pulse rate rising to less than a hundred and fifty.

Sue Tulloh – training on the road is good, and so is the mountain bike

Secrets of the heart

The secret of success in running (and in most other things) is "know thyself". If you know what your limits are you can set yourself the right targets in racing and training and you can try to extend those limits. The heart monitor is really useful here, because it tells you exactly what is going on inside.

The intensity of your training can be guaged by your heart rate. It is easy enough to measure the pulse rate at rest, but impossible to do so while running unless you have a heart monitor. We used to take pulse rates, manually, for ten seconds immediately after doing a bit of interval work, but it is difficult to be accurate. There is a general guideline which says that your maximum heart rate should be 220 minus your age, but individuals differ enormously. One person's 'comfortable' heart rate is another's 'threshold' rate. Some people can never get their heart rate up to 160, while others have a maximum of over 190 and can run for miles at a rate of over 160.

A lot of people just run as they feel, and you can plan your training entirely along those lines, categorizing your pace as 'easy', 'steady', 'brisk', 'fast' and 'very fast'. In terms of racing speed, 'steady' is probably your marathon pace, 'brisk' is your Threshold (10-mile) pace and 'fast' is your 5k or 10k race pace. 'Very fast' is when your are accumulating lactic acid very quickly; it is somewhere around your one-mile race pace.

The trouble with this method is that you can never find out whether you are gettng fitter or not, because you have no accurate record of either your speed or your effort level. Races are your only guide.

Measuring heart rate

The best way of doing this is by using a heart rate monitor, but you can take your pulse rate easily by finding either the artery in your wrist, just above the ball of the thumb, or one of the arteries in your neck, either side of your windpipe. Time the number of beats per minute at rest, sitting down; time the pulse rate again after you have warmed up, before you start the timed run, and then take it once again as soon as possible after you have finished.

Using a heart monitor you can easily measure your pulse rate at rest, when walking and when jogging ('easy' pace). If you run round your fixed course (1–2 miles), timing yourself, at a 'steady' pace and later at a brisk pace, you will then have heart rates for different levels of performance.

To get an accurate measure of your maximum heart rate, you should do a thorough warm-up and then do two flat-out runs of about 3 minutes, with only 3 minutes recovery. You will reach your maximum heart rate by the last minute of the second run. If you have a track handy, do it as a 2 x 800m time trial, trying to run as fast as possible on the first run and trying to equal the speed on the second go.

You now have a set of measurements looking something like this:

Heart Rate	beats per minute
Resting	64
Walking	85
Jogging	110
Brisk running	150–160 (after 3 minutes and after 10 minutes)
Maximum	180

Your range of pulse rate is 116 (the difference between 'resting' and 'maximum') so...

- '50% effort' would be 64 (resting) + 58 (50% of 116) which is 122
- '75% effort' would be 64 + 87, which is 151
- '90% effort' would be 64 + 105,which is 169

Effective training paces

For building endurance and for your recovery runs you will be running at no more than 50% effort.

For improving your running speed you have got to be training at between 75% and 95% effort. To relate these efforts to your performance in races:

- 75% effort corresponds to 'threshold pace' (our ten-mile pace)
- 90% effort corresponds to your 10km race pace
- 95% effort corresponds to your 5km race pace

The hard-training athlete will probably put in three hard sessions a week, one at each of these paces, so that he will be working on a 'hard-easy-hard-easy'-pattern, with a long slow run on the seventh day. For those in the 45–55 age range, two hard sessions a week is probably enough and for the over–55s, one hard session and one long run per week.

The runs at threshold pace may be done without a break, following a warm-up, or they may be done in sections of ten minutes or so at a time, with very short breaks. This is possible because at this pace oxygen is being taken into the muscles as fast as it is being used up. At the higher intensities, however, the oxygen supply is not sufficient and so an 'oxygen debt' builds up, in the form of lactic acid. This means that the effort cannot be sustained for very long, and recovery periods are necessary. This type of training can be done in three main ways:

- **Fartlek:** This a Swedish word meaning 'speed play'. The athlete runs fast for as long as he wants and then slows down to a jog until he is ready for another fast burst. In a 30-minute Fartlek session the athlete might put in 12–15 bursts, lasting 30-60 seconds, with recovery jogs of 60–90 seconds.
- **Interval Training:** This is the most effective type of training and it is used by most of the worlds best runners. The distance run is fixed – usually a multiple of 400m – and so is the recovery time. A typical session for a distance runner might be 15 x 400m, with 60 seconds jogging recovery between each fast 400. When done on a track, this kind of session tells you exactly how fit you are. A novice runner might start by doing, say, 8 x 400m with a 2 minute recovery jog, and averaging 90 seconds for his fast laps. Week by week he runs them a bit faster until he is averaging 80 seconds a lap. He can then increase his endurance by increasing the number and cutting down on the recovery, going up to 12 x 400m with a 90 second recovery, but running

British Vets 5k championship

them more slowly, say 86 seconds, and then aiming to improve the average speed. Someone aiming at a 5k race would do 4–6km of fast work, whereas a 10k runner might start with 8 x 800m and work up to 10 x 1000m, done at 10k speed or a bit faster. (For typical track sessions, see Chapter 8.)

Interval training does not have to be done on a track. A good session on the road is '1 minute fast, 1 minute slow', repeated ten or a dozen times. One of the favourites is 'pyramids', where you do 30 seconds fast, 30 seconds slow, 1 minute fast. 1 minute slow, 2 minutes fast, 2 minutes slow, 1 minute fast, 1 minute slow, 30 secs fast, 30 secs slow. If you do three of these pyramids during your run you have done 15 minutes of fast work

- **Repetition Training:** This term is normally applied to training over distances lasting 3 minutes or longer. One might do repetition miles, or 5-minute repetitions or even 10-minute reps, with a fixed recovery time. One of Richard Nerurkar's best sessions when training for the marathon was 4 x 3k, with 4–5 minute rest. At the other end of the competitive spectrum, we once saw Phyllis Smith, the 400m runner, do a repetition session before the Olympic Games which consisted of 4 x 200m on grass with 20-minute recoveries.

Robinson's Patent Sausages

Although this training method has been in use for a long time, no one has expounded the principle more elegantly than Professor Roger Robinson, the man who gave it a name, in his book, *Heroes and Sparrows* (pub. South-Western Publishing, New Zealand, 1986). Besides representing both England and New Zealand at cross-country, Roger has won the over-forty section of both the New York and the Boston Marathon, as well as World Veterans titles, so he knows what he is talking about.

In the Sausage session you run for set periods of time, making up the route as you go along. The 'sausages', or efforts, can be of any period of time from 1 to 15 minutes; they can be all of the same size, or they can be mixed, as in a 'pyramid' or 'up and down' session. They can be suited to the marathon, e.g. 4 x 15 minutes, to the 10k, e.g. 6 x 5 mins fast, 3 mins slow, or to the 5k, e.g. alternating one and two-minute efforts, and they are particularly good for cross-country training, because a five-minute fast burst may take you through a variety of terrain.

The sausage session combines the principles of Interval training with the freedom and enjoyment of Fartlek. It is best done in a group, with different people leading each fast burst, but it is also a good way of enlivening a solo run.

Making a training plan

You would probably do best to start with one of the ready-made sessions in the book, attuned to your level of ability, but as you get fitter you should plan your own, because everyone is different – some need more speed training, some need more endurance.

How many miles a week?

The volume of your training is a compromise between what you would like to do, what your body can stand, and how much time you have. Some people put in 10 miles a week of training and race regularly, a lot of club runners put in 30–40 miles a week. Professional distance runners mostly run between 70 and 100 miles a week, and marathon runers up to 150. One of our correspondents, Peter Lea, when training for a 24-hour track race, pushed his training up to 30–35 miles *per day* – over 200 miles a week, at the age of 52, but this is not something we would usually recommend! Another correspondent, Robin Sykes, who is a former professional coach, pointed out that many of his contemporaries who had run huge mileages on the road when they were young were now waiting for hip replacements, while he himself, who trains 2–3 times a week and works on his flexibility, remains fit and active.

> **"I have been training twice a day since the age of 18. Twenty years ago I would average around 110 miles a week, now (at 45) it is between 70 and 80 miles a week."**
>
> MICK McGEOCH

The volume of the training, in terms of so many miles per week or hours per week, must be related first of all to what you have done in the past. Whatever your ambitions may be, it's no good launching into a 50 mile a week plan if you have not gone over 25 a week for the last six months. Aim to increase your weekly mileage by no more than 5 miles a week or 10% of the pevious week, whichever is the greater, until you get up to your target.

What speed should I be running at?

Introduce 'quality' sessions after two or three weeks of steady running, starting with one Fartlek session a week, then adding one interval or repetition session a week. For most veterans, two quality sessions a week is plenty. If you want to work harder, work to a 3-day cycle – Easy, Moderate, Hard, with an interval-type session on the Hard days and a brisk run at Threshold (ten-mile) pace on the Moderate days.

Relate your training pace to the pace of your planned races – if you want to race over 10k, do one session a week at 10k pace, and change your programme every three or four months.

Training guidelines

1. Analyse your motives for running.
2. Keep a training diary.
3. Redefine your objectives year by year.
4. Run for enjoyment.
5. Run some races.
6. Join a running club.
7. Get a coach.
8. Look after yourself.
9. Look for variety.
10. Be flexible.

What are you running for?

It is not just the running which matters, it is what you think about when you are running. There are many reasons for taking up running. Let us take a few hypothetical characters, all of them around forty years old, examine their motives and estimate their chances of success.

Howard B. Grate wants to run for his country. He has been a runner since schooldays and joined the local harriers as a teenager. He has always been good; he has won many local road races but he has never reached international level. As he has gets older and his friends have retired, he has continued to train. Now he is eyeing the veteran ranking lists. This is his chance to win a national title and run for his country.

Molly Meanswell worries about what other people think. Some of her friends belong to a gym and they have decided to get fit for a Women's 10k race, to raise funds for a good cause. Molly has never done any running before, but it is such a good cause – and she doesn't want to let he friends down – and think of the good it will be doing her!

Steve Welldunn is a natural sportsman. Even at thirty-nine he is slim, flexible, a squash player, a good dancer, turns out for the firm's cricket-team and ocasionally for the five-a-side team. It was while playing football, in fact, that he noticed that he was puffing a lot more than he did last time he played. When he mentioned this in the bar afterwards, his friend said to him: "what do you expect? You can't expect to keep up with young Robinson – he's about twenty years younger than you." That was it. Steve had always been used to being the best at every sport without trying particularly hard and he wasn't going to accept being beaten by someone younger. He resolved to take up running and get fit.

Wendy Wate-Loess is not at all sporty, but she does like to look good on the dance floor, and in the last few years the weight has crept up. She has read that running is one of the best ways of losing weight and somebody in her road has started a women's 'meet and train' group. She is worried that the others will be a lot better than her.

Peter Pan, the keep-fit man, is not much good at ball-games either, but he is very organised, very disciplined. He watches his diet, swims twice a week and has a subscription to a gym, where he does two thirty-minute sessions a week. Lately, though, he's been finding the routine a bit boring and wondering if there might not be other things in life.

What they don't know, and we don't know either, is whether they enjoy running and whether they are any good at it.

Our long-term goals, the dreams and ambitions, push us into running, but we need short-term goals to keep things going, and these short-term goals should be achievable targets. If you say to yourself: "By this time next year I want to be able to run 10 miles/a stone lighter/under 45 minutes for 10k", you should then say: "In ten weeks time I want to be able to run two miles/3 pounds lighter/running 30 miles a week. When you reach the first target, you set the next one, no longer than three months ahead.

Keep a training diary

BRUCE: "I started my training diary on my twenty-first birthday. I used an ordinary lined exercise book, with one line per day to record the details – the time or distance run, the type of training, i.e. steady run, interval training, Fartlek, the details of times, the weather, and how I felt. The latter is very important. If the comments, day after day, read 'good', or 'felt easy', or 'good and hard', then you will have no problem, but if the remarks start to read: 'tired', 'felt sluggish', 'legs dead', then you are overdoing it and need to ease off before you get injured."

The training diary is an essential part of your running; it is your conscience and your coach. If you want to know how fit you are now compared to six months ago, look at your training diary. How many times a week were you running? How long did you take to get round your regular circuits?

If you want to find out why you are not getting such good results, look at your diary. Do you realise that this is your sixth race in seven weeks and you haven't had much time for training?

If you want to know whether you are ready to run a marathon, look at your diary. How many runs of over two hours have you done in the last ten weeks?

Redefine your objectives year by year

In your first year of running you will make a lot of progress. The things which once seemed a challenge, like running for half an hour without stopping, have become routine.

You now have to decide whether you want to go further or whether you are quite happy with what you have achieved and just want to stay at that level. Even if the latter is the case, you still need to plan your year. Routine running – say a regular twenty miles a week – is OK, but boring routine is not OK. A slight alteration in your plans, season by season, will provide the stimulus to make your training purposeful.

Run for enjoyment

Fun and Fitness should always be the keynotes. Sometimes you may have to work quite hard to achieve your goals, but the pleasure you get from achieving them will make up for the pain. Running should add enjoyment to your life, not restrict it. Enjoy the freedom of being a runner, of being in control, of being strong and fit. Enjoy the changing seasons, the freshness of the morning, the wind in your face. Whatever speed you run, feel glad that you are able to do it.

Run some races

If you have an ounce of competitive spirit in you, you will enjoy running against other people, because there will always be someone you can beat. If you are that perfect Buddha-like individual who hates to beat others because it would demean them, you can enjoy running with other people, helping each other to achieve your personal goals. Both attitudes are a great help during the race. The adrenaline which you produce when there are others running around you will help you to run much faster than you thought was possible. Races give you fixed points in your training year, special days to peak for. Without something to work towards it is difficult to maintain one's enthusiasm.

> **"I don't structure my training at all. If I feel good, I run fast and if I feel tired, I run slowly."**
>
> JENNY MILLS

Join a running club

Some people are clubbable, some are not. Runners tend to be individualists, but that should not prevent you from joining a club. You can get as much or as little from it as you want. At the very least, you will meet people who run regularly and you should be able to find some congenial training partners.

The easiest ways of finding a running club are:

1. **Go to the nearest running shoe shop** and ask.
2. **Look in your local newspaper** for news of running and maybe ring the sports desk to find the contacts.
3. **Go to a local road race** and ask people there.
4. **Buy *Runner's World*** and see what events are on locally.

5. **Get onto the Web** and log onto British-Athletics.com. They have full lists of clubs, most of which have websites.
6. **Write to the appropriate Area Association** (see Appendix 4 for useful addresses). If you live in a city, there may be several clubs within driving range. It is a good idea to visit two or three in your area and find out what they are like. There are really two main types – the long-established club which is very much into serious competition in road, cross-country and track running and the 'new wave' club whose focus is more on running for fitness and enjoyment. Of course there is a lot of overlap; the big clubs often have a joggers section and the new clubs may produce a seriously competitive group, but every club has its own attitude. Some will pressurise you to run in inter-club events – cross-country mob matches, veteran relays – and others never bother to enter a team in anything at all. We suggest that you run with your new club for a few weeks before actually signing up, thus saving recrimination if you don't see eye-to-eye. The things you should ask are:
   - Do they have a running track?
   - Do they have any indoor training facilities?
   - Do they have any coaches?
   - Do they have any social organisation ?

7. **Get a coach.** We all need someone to share our problems with. Unless you have the perfect partner, you cannot expect him/her to have the same enthusiasm for all your interests. The coach does not have to be someone with a coaching certificate or an England tracksuit – just someone with a bit more experience than you, who is prepared to give you time to talk about your running. We go on learning all the time. The important thing is that the coach understands what your goals are in running and values what you do.
8. **Look after yourself.** Remember that you get the benefits of a training session in the recovery period after the session. You expend a lot of energy and lose a lot of fluid when training hard, so get a drink and some carbohydrate food as soon as possible after training. Arrange things so that you have time for a warm-down and a shower after training.

   Bear in mind that the older runner cannot get away with things in the way that the young can. Your rate of production of growth hormones is probably lower than it was, so the adjustment and the recovery after hard training will take a bit longer. Give yourself time to stretch after training. Never put in a hard session until you have rcovered from the previous one.

9. **Look for variety.** This applies to both training and racing. Boredom is the runners enemy, and much as we love our sport, it is all too easy to get into a training rut of doing the same runs week by week. There are lots of different events all over the country every week. Wherever you go in the world you can find fellow-runners and new places to run.
10. **Be flexible.** This means mental flexibility and well as physical. Both are essential. You should certainly work on physical flexibility, by warming up and doing loosening exercises before training and stretching exercises after training. The mental flexibility applies to your ability to adjust your training to the demands of life. We think that the body works to a weekly budget. You don't have to do your training sessions in exactly the same order as the schedule says, but you should try to fit them in at some time in the week. If you do less one day, don't worry about it, but try to compensate later on.

Douglas Cowie

age: **48** occupation: **instructor at sports centre**

"I joined the RAF at the age of 17 and at that time I was a footballer and squash player, but that changed when I met a runner called Bob Wallis, who was coach to Steve Jones. I was coached by Bob for nine years and became a committed runner. I was privileged to be part of an all-international RAF squad during the late seventies and eighties, and we enjoyed great success.

"The team included people like Steve Jones, Ray Crabb, Roger Clark, Roger Hackney and Julian Goater. Mixing with those guys was all the motivation I required! I was introduced to marathons by Donald McGregor, and I ran thousands of miles with him. For twenty years, from the age of 25 until I was 45, an average week in the winter involved racing on Wednesdays and Saturdays and training twice a day on the other days, except for Sundays which was a two to two-and-a-half hour run. We would do a hill session every week, and a repetition session, such a 4 x 5 minutes. The total would be over 80 a week, sometimes 90." (This was the same routine which brought Steve Jones to 8th place in the Olympic 10000m and a world marathon record a few months late –Ed.)

On this training, Douglas Cowie became RAF marathon champion at the age of 30, with 2 hr 23:41, and four years later he ran his PB, 2 hr 21, in the Paris marathon, a feat which earned him a GB international vest, to go with his numerous appearances for Scotland. As a member of the RAF team he competed all over the world – Berlin. Boston, Scandinavia, Paris, Montreal, Ottowa and Washington, After leaving the RAF he started work at the local sports centre, which gave him the opportunity to swim regularly, and at the age of 45 he joined his local cycling club, which involved racing or time-trialling regularly in the summer. By combining the different sports he has worked out a comprehensive, though demanding, training system. (See Chapter 7)

"At the moment I feel as fit and healthy as I have ever done in my life. I am convinced that this is due to 'cross training'. I swim three times a week; I do lengths with a buoy, doing 'arms only'. It tones up the upper body, but the benefit I've felt most in my running is controlled breathing.

"So far I have done 48 marathons and I want to to 50 before my 51st birthday – the World Vets in Kuala Lumpur in 2003 would be a good one. I also intent to retire from competition and finish at the top – healthy! But, on saying that, I can't ever see myself not running. I've always fancied orienteering. Who knows?"

Just before going to press, Douglas won the Scottish Veterans marathon title

CHAPTER SIX
The fitness programme

"A bear, however hard he tries, grows tubby without exercise"

A A MILNE

You are approaching your fortieth birthday. You can't get into the trousers you wore ten years ago. You find that running about with your children leaves you breathless after a remarkably short time. In a word, you want to get fit. Your programme starts with Stage One.

On the other hand, you may be quite fit already, playing football or squash in the winter, cricket or tennis in the summer, but you want to give running a try. Your programme starts at Stage Two.

This is for those who are starting from scratch, with no running background. Those who have already done some running can glance through it and feel smug, but if they are impatient to get on we suggest they move straight to Chapter 7.

The pleasure and the pain

Let's face this 'enjoyment versus pain' thing right from the start. Running really hard is painful and running moderately hard is moderately uncomfortable, but you don't keep it up it for very long and when you have done it you feel terrific. Running at an easy pace, talking pace, is no harder than walking when you are fit and, like walking, a long run is good fun. At 66, Bruce can still go out for an

Anyone can run

eight-mile run and say 'that was lovely'. Unlike swimming in a pool or training in a gym, you can choose where you run, run different routes according to the weather and usually find something to stimulate your mind as well as your body. Even when the scenery is familiar, the sensation of running, of being in control, is pleasurable. It has been shown that running for a long time causes the release of endorphins in the brain; these improve your mood and can even cure depression. Mind you, the harder you run, the more quickly you get tired and the sensations of fatigue and pain will override the pleasant sensations. The last ten minutes might be quite hard work, but to counterbalance that there is the satisfaction of being able to do an eight-mile run and the pleasure of anticipating a nice shower afterwards, a rest and a drink.

Of course you could get up from in front of the television and have a shower, a rest and a drink, but it would not be nearly so satisfying. You cannot enjoy food without some hunger or drink without some thirst, and you cannot enjoy rest unless you have made some effort.

The person who has not run since schooldays will almost certainly find it uncomfortable. The secret is to start at a point on the programme where the exercise is comfortable and enjoyable. When you get used to that level of exercise and can handle it easily, and not until then, you can move up to the next stage.

It's not where you start that matters, as much as where you finish. As long as you keep your original intention in your mind you have a reason for going out running. The problems only arise when your ambition is too great for your level of fitness.

Take Wendy Wate-Loess, for example. Because she is just aiming to take off a few pounds, it doesn't matter how fast she goes or how many miles she does per week, as long as she gradually increases the dose. You will find the relationship between exercise and weight loss in Chapter 12, but she might start off by doing six miles of walking and jogging per week. When she gets up to ten miles a week she will be able to see tangible results, and she won't need to do any more to achieve her goal. Howard B. Grate, however, has ideas of running a marathon, and since this demands at least six months preparation he may find that his enthusiasm runs out before he is in sight of his goal.

Satisfaction comes when your achievements match your ambitions. If your short-term goals are modest and attainable, you will get more fun out of the sport. Molly Meanswell just wants to get round the 10k race with her friends, so she will be happy to finish, however long it takes her. Peter Pan, with a cautious methodical approach, will run his first race with a bit in hand and use this as a basis for future training, regardless of his position. Steve Welldunn, on the other hand, accustomed to being a success in every sport, might find it difficult to adjust to being beaten by older men who have more training behind them.

Stage One: the pre-running programme

Do I need a check-up?

Because walking and running are natural activities, there is no need for a medical check-up except in special circumstances. You should ask your doctor for a check-up if:

- You have had a serious operation or a serious illness in the last six months.
- You are over forty and you have a family history of heart disease.
- You are seriously overweight (see Chapter 2).
- You have taken no exercise in the last five years.

What should I wear?

Because we start with walking, no special clothing is necessary. Your shoes should be wide enough for your foot to spread out fully and should not have a high heel. Your clothing should be comfortable as well as suitable for the climate. There is no point in wearing a heavy woollen track-suit in the height of summer or going out in skimpy shorts and singlet on a cold winter's day. As most people are shy about taking exercise when they start, it is best to wear inconspicuous everyday clothing. See Chapter 4 for more details

> **Getting started**
>
> **"I started running at 48. It took me three months of alternating walking and jogging before I could jog continuously for 3 miles. Five years later I ran the London Marathon in 3 hours 12 minutes."**
>
> RALPH HENLEY

How far should I go?

How much you are capable of doing depends on what you are doing at the moment. We start with a fairly gentle walking programme, so if you are already used to walking 2 miles a day you can skip the first two weeks. However, it is best to err on the side of safety, so stick to the programme and don't increase your distance until you feel ready to do so.

Similarly, when you feel you are doing enough for your needs, you don't have to move up just because the programme says so. If running 10 miles a week makes you fit enough for your purposes, just stay on that level.

We have set an arbitrary figure of twenty miles a week for the "full fitness" programme, but the "serious runner" programme will take you up to 30–40 miles a week and the "marathon runner" will take you even further, if that is where you want to go. It's a free country.

How often should I take exercise?

The programme starts with walking every other day, then moves to four and five days a week. Later on, the running programme will do the same. In general, the principle of one day on, one day off, is a sound one. More is not always better.

Should I be on my own?

It is much easier to take exercise if you have someone to keep you company, and if you have made a rendezvous with someone you are much less likely to put off the session because it raining or something. For women, particularly, running in groups engenders confidence and encourages the beginner. If you can't find a friend or relation, put up a card in the local gym or leisure centre and start a 'meet and train' group once or twice a week.

However, one of running's main attractions as a form of exercise is that you don't need twenty-one other players and a referee. If you feel like it, just go out and run. Until you get to know the area, stick to well-lit routes and tell people where you are going.

The programme

Week One

Aim:	to walk 8 miles (or two-and-a-half hours) in the week
Frequency:	Three or four walks in seven days
Speed:	Whatever you feel like

Week Two:

Aim:	To walk 10 miles (or three hours) in the week
Frequency:	Four or five walks in seven days
Speed:	Alternate brisk walks and easy walks

Week Three

Aim:	To walk 12 miles (or three and-a-half hours) in the week
Frequency:	Four or five walks in the seven days
Speed:	Alternate brisk walks and easy walks

Week Four

Aim:	To walk 14 miles (or four hours) in the week
Frequency:	Five walks in seven days
Speed:	On your longer walks, try walking for 15 min easily, then for 15 minutes briskly then easing off again

Develop the habit of using the first part of any session as a warm-up and the last part as a warm-down.

Additional exercise

Stretching and mobility work. All serious runners warm up and loosen up before they start training – particularly in cold climates – and most of them stretch after the running is over, because by then your muscles will be warmer and more flexible. You don't need a warm-up before walking, but after the walking we recommend spending a few minutes on general mobility exercises. We suggest you follow a routine of six to eight simple exercises, spending only 30 seconds on each one – for example: arm swinging, shoulder rotation, hip rotation, side bending, deep knee bends, leg swinging, toe touching and sit-ups (see Appendix 1).

What about gym work?

If you have access to a gym, there is no reason why you should not increase your level of fitness by spending 15-30 minutes, twice a week, following a general strength-building programme.A good programme would involve three weight-training exercises for arms and shoulders, one each for back and abdominal muscles and three for leg strength including work for both the 'quads' at the front of the thighs and the hamstrings at the back of the thighs (see Appendix 2).

The other way in which you can use your gym in the early stages is to monitor your fitness by using one of the cycling or treadmill exercises linked to a heart monitor. Choose a test just above the low end of the range for your first try, so that you are not over-stressing yourself, and measure your heart-rate during ten minutes of steady activity, e.g. treadmill at 5 miles an hour (8 km/h) on a 1% slope. Doing this once a week during Stages One and Two and you will see a marked improvement. What was moderately strenuous will become easy and your heart rate will not go up as much. The next step is to select a programme a couple of notches higher and see how your running training affects that.

Aches and Pains (see Chapter 13)

Doing something different is bound to cause a reaction, so even regular walking may cause stiffness to start with, particularly if you are changing from high-heeled to low-heeled shoes.

The Portsmouth '5'

Stiffness is one of the body's safety-precautions, so don't ignore it. If you are walking every other day, the stiffness should be wearing off by the second day. Start slowly and gently, and if the stiffness gets worse, turn around and wait another day. Your motto should be: "if in doubt, ease off". If the stiffness is really painful, take an anti-inflammatory such as Ibuprofen or Aspirin.

The other pain you may encounter is shin soreness, caused by the impact on hard surfaces. The solution to this is to get off the road and onto the grass as often as possible. This is where the benefits of 'cross training'- come in, using swimming, cycling and gym work, all of which are low-impact sports which improve your strength and your fitness.

Stage Two: Beginners' running programme

Getting more from less

Once you have got used to getting out and walking for three or four hours a week, you should have no problem with the running, because it takes less time. A brisk walk is four miles an hour, at least fifteen minutes per mile on a flat path. Jogging a mile slowly will take you about ten minutes, and when you get fitter it will be only eight minutes, so you are covering the ground and burning up the calories at almost twice the speed. Moreover, because the demand on the heart and lungs is greater, you are getting more fitness benefit from half an hour of running than from an hour of walking.

When to run

The best time is always before meals – you should not try running on a full stomach. Many people find that before breakfast is the only time they can guarantee having to themselves, but it takes some getting used to, and most of us perform better later in the day. If you have somewhere to shower and change, a half-hour session before lunch is excellent. Daylight is guaranteed and you often get the best part of the day.

When not to run

You should not run if you have a temperature more than 1°C above normal (do you know what your normal temperature is? Not everyone is 37°C)

You should not run after an illness, until given clearance by your doctor.

You should not run if you are feeling sick (unless it's a race-day, when it is just nerves!)

If you are just feeling very tired, or headachy, or a bit stiff, put your kit on and go for a walk.If you start to feel better, jog gently.Often running itself will clear up your symptoms.

A slight cold in the head need not stop, you, as long as you have proper clothing, but do not run if you have a chest cold, cough or sore throat.

Where to run

The best places are parks, playing fields, footpaths and beaches, but any quiet stretch of road will do. If you want to find out how fast you are running, go to a public running track. They are all 400m tracks, which means 4 laps to the mile.

How fast should I go?

In the early stages – the first four weeks of running, at any rate, don't run above 'talking pace'. If you start to feel very breathless, either drop to a walk for thirty seconds or just slow down the pace until it feels comfortable again. This is what is meant by 'walk-jog'.

It takes time for your body to get used to continuous running, but it will adjust, believe us, as long as you give it time.

The Programme

Week One	
Aim:	to get out four times
Day 1:	10 mins walking, 10 mins walk-jog, 10 mins walk
Day 2:	5 mins walk, 15 mins walk-jog, 5 mins walk
Day 3:	As Day 1
Day 4:	A three-mile circuit, jogging and walking as you feel

Week Two	
Aim:	to run four times
Day 1:	5 mins walk, then 6 x 1 min jog, one minute walk
Day 2:	5 mins walk, 20 mins walk-jog
Day 3:	5 mins walk, 10 mins continuous run, 5 mins walk
Day 4:	As Week One, but with less walking

Week Three	
Aim:	to run 6 miles in a week
Day 1:	5 mins warm-up, then 8 x 1 min jog, 30 secs walk
Day 2:	5 mins walk, 15 mins jog-walk or 30 mins cycling
Day 3:	5 mins walk, 5 mins jog, 2 mins walk, 5 mins jog
Day 4:	5 mins warm-up, 2 mile jog with short walking breaks

Week Four	
Aim:	to run a mile non-stop
Day 1:	As Week Three, but increase to 10 x 1 min jog
Day 2:	15 mins jog-walk or 30 mins cycling
Day 3:	4 miles brisk walking, with occasional jogging
Day 4:	5 mins walk, 2 mins stretch, then a timed jog of 1 mile

Week Five

Aim:	to run 8 miles in a week
Day 1:	5 mins warm-up, then 4 x 2 mins jog, 1 min walk
Day 2:	2 miles approx, jogging most of the way
Day 3:	5 mins walk, 6 mins jog, 2 mins walk, 6 mins jog
Day 4:	3 miles circuit, jogging most of the time

Week Six

Aim:	to run 8 miles in a week
Day 1:	5 mins warm-up, then 4 x 2 mins and 4 x 1 min jog, 1 min walk
Day 2:	15 mins jog, walk when necessary
Day 3:	5 mins walk, 2 mins stretch, one mile steady pace, untimed
Day 4:	Go round your 4-mile circuit, running most of the time

Week Seven

Aim:	to run a timed mile
Day 1:	Warm-up for 5 mins, then 4 x 3 mins jog, l min walk
Day 2:	5 mins easy, 2 mins stretching, 15 mins steady pace
Day 3:	15 mins jog
Day 4:	5 mins walk, 5 mins jog, 2 mins stretching, then run a mile as Week Four and time it, then jog-walk for 5 more minutes

Week Eight

Aim:	to run 10 miles in the week
Day 1:	10 mins out slowly, then run back faster
Day 2:	5 mins easy, then 8–10 x 1 min fast, 1 min slow
Day 3:	20 mins jog
Day 4:	Do a mile of warm-up, then go round your 4-mile circuit, as Week 6

Keeping records

To start with, the simplest thing is to copy this plan, pin it up somewhere and either tick it off or write in what you actually do. When you get into running regularly, keep a training diary.

What about missed days?

It does not matter about doing the days in the correct order, as long as you put in the four days. If you miss a single day in a week, carry on as normal, but

Ann Ridley – hard effort brings results

if you have missed two days, so that you have only run twice that week, repeat the week before moving up to the next.

Do other sports make me fitter?

This is all tied up with your reason for running. Some people take up running to get fit for other sports, like football or hockey, so, obviously, a couple of days a week will be taken up doing those sports, to which you will add your two or three days of independent training.

If we are trying to control the overall training load, these other sports have to be taken into account. We generally reckon that an hour of a team sport is equivalent to four miles of running. With individual sports like tennis it depends on the effort level. A brisk half-hour of singles might be worth 3–4 miles of running, but half an hour of doubles would only be worth 2–3 miles.

Doing other things, like weight training or swimming, will certainly help your all-round fitness, but perhaps the question you meant to ask is: will doing other sports affect my running? Most coaches would agree that a weekly or twice-weekly weight-training session, added on to your running programme, would make you a better runner, but for the average person, running 3 or 4 times a week, doing a weight session instead of a running session would not. Certainly we do not advise doing a weight session or another sport the day before a race.

Cross-training is one of today's buzz-words. It means training for one sport by doing another. Sports which make large demands on the heart-lung system and involve the same muscle-groups as running can be used to good effect. The advantages are, firstly, that they reduce the chances of injury caused by the impact of running on roads and, secondly, that they add variety to the training regime. Cycling, rowing and cross-country skiing are the best examples. The cycling is more effective if done on a mountain bike on hilly courses. All three of these sports can be done on a machine in the gym. A sample cross-training schedule can be found in the next chapter.

Colin Dow

age: **52** occupation: **sports centre manager**

Colin Dow has not won any world titles, but he epitomises the thousands of people who run for fitness and enjoyment. He is one of the driving forces behind the Marlborough Running Club, of which it is said: "at the present rate of increase the club numbers should reach 225,000 by the middle of the century" (the population of the town is 10,000) and also: "this is a drinking club with a running problem."

"I started running when I was in my late twenties, mainly as a means of keeping fit for squash. However, I soon found myself caught up in the marathon mania of the 1980s. It seemed in those days that running the marathon was the ultimate achievement which everyone wanted. Everybody remembers their first marathon; mine was in Cardiff and I remember sitting on the roadside at the finish in total Utopia, having run under 3 hr 30.

"Over the next few years I continued running marathons and evenutally achieved a best time of just under three hours, only to be told that the course was short! For a change I started to compete in triathlons and enjoyed the multi-discipline aspect of the sport. When I moved to Wiltshire and didn't have the time for triathlon training I discovered the joys of trail running, particularly long distance stuff, which is still my main enjoyment. To be up on the hills and running gives me a buzz I don't get with road running.

"Memorable moments are many: finishing the South Downs run (80 miles), breaking the ice before getting in to swim in the 'Tough Guy', and having a sprint finish with my team mate at the end of the Otter Peak 40-miler. But the best was definitely finishing my first marathon.

"I still run most days, but also mix it with a bit of off-road cycling. I have decided that as I am not going to get any faster I might as well take my time and enjoy the experience. I don't feel I have to run every day, but if I don't manage to get out for a few days I miss it. For the future I hanker after one more big long distance run, such as the West Highland Way, but if I can't manage the training time I will still be happy as long as I can get out into the countryside – and run."

CHAPTER SEVEN

The full fitness programme

The object of this programme is to stay fit and healthy for the rest of your life.

BRUCE: "As I write this, and I know that it is tempting fate, I haven't stopped running regularly since I took a few weeks off in the summer of 1955. OK, so I am naturally skinny and built for running, but in several decades of teaching and coaching I must have been exposed to an awful lot of germs. The reason that I have never been seriously ill may be partly genetic, but I like to think that staying fit and eating well has given me a robust immune system."

Following a sound fitness programme does not guarantee that you will never get ill, but it does stack the odds in your favour. A good fitness programme must provide the following benefits:

1. It keeps your weight down.
2. It gives you a strong cardiovascular system.
3. It maintains your flexibility.
4. It maintains a good level of all-round muscular strength.

A runner's fitness programme should also make you fit enough to run in a 10k race. This gives it a different slant to a fitness programme based around a gym or a pool.

You won't be as strong in the arm as someone who does weight-training and you won't be as flexible as someone who does Yoga four times a week – but you will be able to run a lot faster than them.

The programme which follows is one which can be safely followed up to the age of fifty and maybe beyond. Those who have the desire and the talent may wish to go on to the more strenuous programmes in the later chapters – the marathon schedules for example, but this one will make you fit enough to run a respectable 10k.

Age adjustments

The programme you are following at 45 will probably not be the right one for you at 65.

During those twenty years, in spite of your best efforts, you will have lost some flexibility and some muscle strength. You will not be running as fast, as we have seen in Chapter 1. We have therefore suggested, throughout the book, some guidelines for modifying the tougher programmes.

Running only schedule

Week 1	
Day 1:	3 miles easy run
Day 2:	1 mile jog, then 5 x 1 min brisk, 1 min jog, 5 mins easy jog
Day 3:	3 miles steady pace
Day 4:	4-5 miles easy, walking if necessary
Week's total:	13-14 miles

Week 2	
Day 1:	3-4 miles easy pace
Day 2:	Warm-up, 6 x 30 secs uphill fast, walking back, 1 mile jog
Day 3:	Warm-up 1 mile, then timed run, 2 miles approx, 5 mins jog
Day 4:	5 miles easy, off-road
Week's total:	15–16 miles

"I started running when I was informed that I was going to become a father, I was overweight and had been smoking since the age of 12. To begin was torture, but I persevered and became a competent marathon runner."

JONATHAN SUCH (WHO LATER RAN THE 90KM COMRADES MARATHON IN UNDER 7 HOURS)

Week 3

Day 1:	4 miles easy pace
Day 2:	1 mile easy, 8 x 30 secs fast, 1 min jog, warm-down
Day 3:	Warm up, 3 miles brisk pace
Day 4:	5 miles easy, off-road
Week's total:	16-17 miles

Week 4

Day 1:	4 miles steady pace
Day 2:	1 mile warm-up, 4 miles steady, inc. 6 x 1 min fast bursts
Day 3:	Timed run as Week 2
Day 4:	5–6 miles endurance run, off-road
Week's total:	18–19 miles

Week 5

Day 1:	5 miles easy pace
Day 2:	2M easy, 6 x 1 min fast, 2 mins slow, 1 mile easy
Day 3:	4 miles steady pace
Day 4:	6 miles endurance run,starting slowly
Week's Total:	20 miles

Week 6

Day 1:	5 miles easy
Day 2:	6 miles steady, inc. 8 x 30 secs fast
Day 3:	5 miles steady pace
Day 4:	10 mins warm-up, 10 mins brisk pace, 5 mins jog, 10 mins brisk, 10 mins jog
Week's total:	22 miles approx.

Week 7

Day 1:	6 miles easy, off road
Day 2:	1 mile jog, 10 x (1 min fast, 2 mins slow), 1 mile easy
Day 3:	Warm up, 3 x 5 mins fast, 4 mins recovery, 1 mile jog
Day 4:	8 miles endurance run
Week's total:	25 miles

Week 8	
Day 1:	6 miles easy, with 6 x 100m stride at the end
Day 2:	6 miles Fartlek, as Week 6, with 10 x 30 secs bursts
Day 3:	5 miles easy
Day 4:	Warm up, Race 4–7 miles or 5 miles fast, timed
Week's total:	25 miles

Week 9	
Day 1:	7 miles, easy pace
Day 2:	Warm up, 8 x 400m, timed, 2 mins recovery
Day 3:	4 miles steady pace
Day 4:	6 miles Fartlek, alternating 1 min and 2 mins bursts
Week's total:	23 miles

Week 10	
Day 1:	Warm up, 12 x (200m fast stride, 1 min rest), 1 mile jog
Day 2:	5 miles easy
Day 3:	20 mins jogging, inc. 6 x 150m fast stride
Day 4:	RACE (5 miles–10k)

Notes	
Easy pace:	able to talk easily while running
Steady pace:	marathon speed – still able to talk
Brisk pace:	threshold pace or ten-mile race pace – little breath to spare
Fartlek:	fast bursts at 5K race speed, with periods of easy running in between

Age Adjustments

At ths level it is the state of fitness which counts, rather than the age. The final workload is twenty-five miles a week – about three hours a week, which is not excessive for a sixty or even a seventy-year-old runner. The key is to move up to the next week only when you are confident that you can handle it. If other pressures get in the way, stay at, say, Week 4, for three weeks before breaking the 20-miles-a-week barrier. There is no hurry – you have the rest of yout life.

Additional Training

If you are already doing other forms of exercise, such as swimming or weight training, we suggest that you try to keep them going while you are building up your running. If not, do not add anything until you have adjusted to the extra workload.

After that you might consider what else you need. Weight training is the easiest thing to do, because it improves all-round muscular strength, which otherwise declines at the rate of about 0.5% per year after the age of 40. See the recommendations in Chapter 9.

Racing cross-country

Sports such as hockey, squash, football all require fitness, but they do not develop fitness to a great extent, because the periods of intense effort tend to be short, interspersed with longer periods of rest or low-level activity. The older the player gets, the more he tends to use his experience to save himself extra effort. This pays off in the short term, because there is still a reserve of energy which can be tapped in an emergency, but in the long term it is self-defeating, because the body is not being pushed. The older games player therefore needs to work on his fitness more between games – with running for cardiovascular fitness, or with weights in the gym for strength, to stay at the same level. He also has to be more aware of the need to warm up and warm down properly.

The weekly sportsman's programme

Day	
Monday	Warm up, 15-20 mins brisk pace, warm down
Tuesday	Club training night plus 20 mins weight training
Wednesday	Six mile run with 20 x 30 second bursts, 60 secs jog
Thursday	45 mins gym work plus 3-mile jog
Friday	Rest
Saturday	Competition
Sunday	60 mins run

The triathlon programme

Swimming and cycling are excellent ways of maintaining cardio-vascular fitness, so when combined with running, making a triathlon, you have an almost perfect training programme

It is probably true to say that triathletes are the fittest section of the population, because they develop the muscles needed for running, swimming and cycling at the same time as building great endurance and a tremendous heart-lung system. The only groups to compare with them are the rowers and the cross-country skiiers, who also use a wide variety of muscles.

The great strength of triathlon training is that it has a much lower proportion of 'impact stress' – the effect of the foot hitting the road time after time. The drawbacks are that to compete you need a good bike (expensive), a safe place to cycle (rare in Britain) and plenty of warm water to swim in (almost unknown in Britain).

However, if you merely want to train like a triathlete and get the benefits, you can use the local pool for your swimming and get a little pair of rollers (the Turbo Trainer) on which you can mount your bike. You can then do a twenty-mile spin on the bike without leaving the house.

Douglas Cowie, the RAF runner (see p. 73) who reached international level in the marathon, now uses the following schedule, at the age of 48:

Day	
Sunday:	90 mins easy run
Monday:	40 mins bike on Turbo Trainer, swim 20 mins, 6 mile run
Tuesday:	7–8 miles hard run with local club
Wednesday:	As Monday
Thursday:	Steady 6 mile run with club
Friday:	As Monday
Saturday:	Race or repetition session, e.g. 4 x 1 mile fast, 3 mins rest

This is a pretty tough programme, involving up to fifty miles a week of running, but up to the age of 45 he was running almost twice as much, and now he says: "I feel as fit and healthy as I have done in my whole life."

Age adjustments

Only very fit 40-somethings could handle this without a rest day. For the majority of over-40s we would recommend that one of the Monday-Wednesday-

World Vets 10k championships

Friday sessions be reduced to 20 mins swim only – which still leaves six days of running. For over-50s we recommend that the Sunday run should be one hour, the Monday-Wednesday sessions be either cycle-swim or run-swim, and the Friday should be rest or swim only.

Seasonal adjustments

- **Winter:** This is out of the competition season, unless you are going off to South Africa or Australia to compete. If the weather and the road conditions make it difficult to run in the evenings, you can still do the indoor cycling and the swimming, but you could substitute a weight training session for the running on Monday and Wednesday nights and concentrate your running on Tuesday, Thursday, Saturday and Sunday. At the weekend you could aim to swim seriously on Saturday morning and put in a hard running session, e.g. 15 x 400m later in the day. On Sunday you can put in a three-hour cycle-run session, altering the balance to suit your needs.

- **Summer:** Training here must be related to competition, always bearing in mind that training is very specific. There is more value in putting in a long cycle ride after a mile swim, and more value in putting in a running session after getting off a bike, even if the bike ride is only a brisk twenty minutes to get the track. In the running sessions, alternate between some form of interval training and brisk 15-30 minutes 'tempo runs'.

The safest way to improve, as in pure running, is to increase the volume first, and only improve the quality of the training once you can handle the quantity.

Jenny Gray

age: **41** occupation: **television producer, mother of two**

"The first time I remember running was when I was eight years old. My father used to stand at the window in our lounge and time my brother and I while we raced about two miles up a country lane and back- we did it almost every evening in the summer months. When I was at school there was no opportunity to do athletics. At university I played a bit of squash and ran three miles around the golf course every morning. My first race was the Durham Colleges Fun Run, 5km, where I was the first woman. While I lived in Japan I tried to do twenty minutes every morning to keep fit, but that stopped when I moved to London.

"During the years that my two children were born I maintained my fitness by going to the gym and doing aerobic classes. We moved to the countrysie in Hertfordshire in 1995 and there was an opportunity to run again; work and children restricted me to running six miles once a week, but I managed three aerobic or weight-training classes a week as well. On that training I ran my first half marathon in 1997, and did it in 1 hr 36. After running a few more races I decided to train for the 1999 London Marathon. I increased my training to one long run a week and two aerobic classes, and ran it in 3 hr 13. After that people said that I should train properly, so I joined my nearest club – Vauxhall AC – and set foot on a track for the first time.

"I started running four times a week, including two sessions on the grass track. My 10k time came down to 39 minutes and then 38:05. I had my first cross-country season and won the Chiltern League series."

Since then, Jenny has gone on to become a highly successful runner in the W40 category – and she is still improving. She ran 3 hr 3 in the 2000 London Marathon and 2 hr 57 in 2001. In 2000 she won her first British Vets track championship at 5000m, with 17:51, and in 2001 she won the British Vets 1500m in 4:43 – her first race at the distance – before going to Australia for the World Veterans Championships and winning bronze medals in both the 5000m (17:40) and the 1500m (4:40).

Typical week's training

Monday:	Track training – 5 x 800m, plus a one mile swim
Tuesday:	Track training – warm-up plus some striding
Wednesday:	Swim 1 mile.
Thursday:	Long slow run, 90–110 minutes
Friday:	Track training – 8 x 300m with a short recovery
Saturday:	Rest
Sunday:	Swim 1 mile

Colm Rothery –
World record holder

CHAPTER 8

Track training

Most people come into running through road racing – perhaps from seeing the London Marathon on TV or being persuaded to join a charity fun run. We have met people on our courses who have never been on a running track. There is a feeling that the running track is only for the young and fit, but this is by no means the case. Tracks tend to be heavily used a couple of evenings a week, when the local club has its training nights, and under-used the rest of the time. You need to check to find out whether the track is being used over the weekend, because some summer weekends are busy.

The good things about running tracks are:

1. You have a reliable, traffic-free all-weather surface to run on.
2. You know exactly how far you are running. A lap on the inside lane is 400m, which means that 4 laps equals a mile (1609m) as near as dammit. If you run a lap in the second lane, you run an extra 8m, in the third lane, an extra 16m, and so on, but there are track markings to allow for this.
3. You usually have changing and toilet facilities handy.
4. It gives you a chance to meet up with other runners.

The drawbacks of running tracks are:

1. You have to pay.
2. Although tracks are softer than roads, too much fast track running can lead to injury.
3. Because you know exactly how far you are running, you can't kid yourself about your state of fitness.

Steve Ovett – world class from 400m to the half marathon

Getting used to the track

You don't have to warm up on the track – often it is better to do that on the grass; this prevents the track becoming clogged up with joggers and it is also easier on your legs. On your first visit I suggest that you do no more than 8 laps. Run four times round in one of the outside lanes, jogging round the bends and accelerating down the straights, gradually working up to a sprinting speed.

Take a breather, stretch a bit, and then try four laps of running 200m fast and jogging slowly for the remainder. Time yourself over 200m, making sure that you start from the right stagger mark for the lane you are in (ask someone about this if you are in doubt).

Next time you come down – at least three days later, repeat the process but drop the four laps of jogging bends, striding straights and do 8 x 200m.

After three sessions of this you will be ready to tackle running full laps. A good start would be to do 4 x 200m, then 4 x 400m, jogging 200m slowly for your recovery.

The basic track session

This is proper interval training, the backbone of training for all serious track runners. You fix the distance to be done, the number of repeats and the recovery time you are going to allow yourself, and then you run them in as fast an average time as possible.

For a start, having gone through the preparation above, we recommend 8 x 400m, with a recovery jog of 200m, for which you allow yourself 2 minutes. The running speed, to start with, should be your 5k speed. If you haven't run a 5k race, divide your 10k time by two and then deduct about 45 seconds. A 40-minute 10k person might expect to do 5k in 19:15, but a 30-minute 10k man would expect

14:30, and a 50-minute 10k runner would expect 24 minutes for 5k. The appropriate 400m pace is shown in Table 4 below.

Table 4: 5000m pace chart

5000m speed (mins:secs)	pace per 400m lap (secs)	5000m speed (mins:secs)	pace per 400m lap (secs)
15:00	72	20:50	100
15:50	76	21:40	104
16:40	80	22:30	108
17:30	84	23:20	112
18:20	88	23:10	116
19:10	92	25:00	120
20:00	96	25:50	124

Progression

You can progress in three different ways – by running them faster, by cutting down the recovery, or by doing more. We suggest that once you have established what you can do for 8 x 400m, you move up to doing 10 at the same pace, with the same recovery. As you get fitter you can cut down the recovery jog to 90 seconds. Week by week your average time should come down. When you feel that you have reached a plateau, go back to doing 8 with a 2-minute recovery, and trying to run them a couple of seconds a lap faster.

This 10 x 400m session, with a shortish recovery, is a very good guide to fitness and can be done anywhere in the world that you can find a track. It tells you exactly where you stand, and it is also good training for anyone running races of 1500m or longer. Where you go from here depends on what your goals are.

Training for middle distance (800-1500m)

1. Training is specific to the event. You have got to become efficient at running at your race pace. The art is in putting all your effort into the two minutes or four minutes of the race, so as you get nearer to competition you will be doing sessions which simulate the stresses of the race.
2. Aerobic training must form the bulk of your work, even if you are running 800 and 1500m. Even in the 800m, more of the energy comes from aerobic rather than anaerobic sources (see Chapter 2). The great 800m runners, like Wilson Kipketer, Peter Snell or Sebastian Coe,

always included a lot of aerobic sessions. You must continue to work on aerobic fitness right up to the start of the main competition period.

3. You also have to run fast. Most races are won and lost over the last 200m, so you have to practise your sprinting technique. Another important point is that only when you are running at your fastest do you fully stimulate the body to produce the necessary hormones.

Getting the right mixture

In your training you should try to cover all the options. You need at least one main aerobic session a week, and one session which is close to your race pace, but you will also need to do some speedwork. This can be done at the end of a steady run, running over 150m, accelerating up to a sprint and then easing down again, but it is best done by practising in the context of 'race rehearsal'. Try running 300m stretches with a friend. One leads at the steady pace of the race and the other sits in and then kicks for the last 100 metres. Another way of doing this is to run 'differential' 400s, where you run the first 200m at race pace and then kick in a fast second 200m, trying to stay as smooth and efficient as possible.

To fit in all these sessions you need to operate on a cycle which is longer than seven days. This could be a ten-day cycle, which would fit in with a major race every three weeks or a 14-day cycle, allowing for a race every two or four weeks.

Basic middle distance session

This would suit an over-40 runner who has already had 8 weeks of training on the track as outlined above.

Weekly pattern:	
Monday:	Endurance work, on grass or on hills
Tuesday:	Track session at 1500m pace
Wednesday:	Rest or easy running
Thursday:	Track session at 800m pace
Friday:	Rest
Saturday:	Minor race or time trial
Sunday:	40–50 mins slow running, off road

All track sessions should be preceded by 15 minutes of warming up and followed by at least five minutes of jogging and five minutes of stretching.

Endurance sessions: 6 x 2 mins on grass (2 mins jog recovery) or 6 x 90 secs uphill.

1500m sessions: 2 x (4 x 400m) at race pace or faster, with 2 mins recovery between each 400m and an extra 2 mins between sets, or pyramid of 200m-400m-600m-800m-600m-400m-200m at race pace, with 60 secs of recovery for each 200m of fast work, i.e. 4 mins recovery after the 800.

800m sessions: 8 x 200m or 5 x 300m or 3 x 400m at race speed, with 2–3 minutes recovery for every 200m of fast work, i.e. 4–6 mins recovery after a fast 400.

Allowances for age. Over 50: do only two of the three sessions down for Tues-Thur-Saturday, substituting an easy jog, gym work or cycling. Over-60: do only one of the three quality sessions, and allow a two or three-day gap between the endurance session and the 1500m or 800m session.

John Seed started running long distances as a 40-year-old in 1980, but ten years later switched to sprinting, running under 30 seconds for 200 metres. Ten years after that, at the age of sixty, he ran a personal best of 28.4 seconds.

Elite middle distance session

This would be suitable for experienced under-50 athletes aiming at championship races. It includes training at a variety of different paces, as follows:

A. Run at your 5000m pace 4 x 1200m or 5 x 1000m, or do a 'pyramid' session of 800-1000-1200-100-800m. The recovery time is 60 secs for every 400m run.

B. Run at your 3000m pace: 5 x 800m or 7 x 600m or 4 x (600m + 400m)

C. Run at your 1500m pace: 10-12 x 400m with 75–90 secs recovery or 3 x (4 x 400m) with 75 secs between runs and 3 mins between sets. Here you aim to run each set slightly faster than the one before.

D. Run at your 800m pace: 6 x 300m or 4 x 400m or pyramid session of 200-300-400-400-300-200m, with 60 secs recovery for every 100m run.

E. Run at your 400m race pace. These would be done in the last phase before competition, otherwise an extra A or B session would be done. 2 x (150-200-300m) or 6 x 200m, with 4–5 mins recovery after each fast run.

In a two week cycle, all of these can be done, with a race or time trial at the end, making six hard sessions in two weeks:

	Week 1	Week 2
Monday:	Easy	E
Tuesday:	A	Easy
Wednesday:	Easy	C
Thursday:	B	Easy
Saturday:	D	RACE DAY

If Sunday is used for a long easy run and Friday is a rest day, the other days of the week can be used for easy recuperation runs, or for Fartlek if you recover quickly.

Allowances for age: over-50: Keep to the same frequency, but reduce the volume of each quality session by one-third and have at least one complete rest day per week. Over-60: Only two quality sessions per week, reduced in volume as for over-50s

Training for 5000m and 10000m

The same principles described for the middle distance runners apply here, but because there is only a small anaerobic element involved in these distances, most of the training is aerobic. However, the speed work and the speed endurance sessions must not be ignored, because these are the ones which have the maximum stimulation effect on the body. The basic track training session will total 5000–6000m of fast work for the 5000m runner, and 8000m to over 10000m of fast work for the serious 10k runner.

Basic 5000m sessions: Interval 400m runs should start at 12 x 400m and work up to 15 x 400m. A good way of doing them is to run 800m followed by a recovery jog and then 400m. Five sets of (800+400m) is less wearing mentally than a full 15 x 400m.

Basic 10000m sessions: The standard distance here is usually 800m or 1000m, so one would do 8–10 reps of these for a full session, but occasionally do 6–8 x 1200m or 4–6 x 1600m.

Age allowances: over-50s need go only up to 12 x 400m or 6 x 1000m, over-60s to 10 x 400m, 5 x 1000m.

Faster reps or shorter rests?

This is one of running oldest controversies, and we suspect that the way people respond depends on temperament as much as on logic. Are you, basically, a Cavalier or a Roundhead?, An Italian or a Swede? There are some people who just love to run fast laps, even if their recovery time is fifteen minutes, while others like to go for high volume, even though their training speed may be slower than their races. The situation, with which we are all familiar, is that you have a standard training session – it might be five times a mile with 3 mins recovery for a serious road runner, or 6 x 800m with 2 mins recovery for a track runner. You started doing them in January, pretty slowly, but by March you were running them almost as fast as your race speed, and by April you were averaging something a little faster than your race speed. Do you aim to run still faster in the next session, on the principle that 'the harder I train, the better I get' or try something else?

Sheila Carey and Pat Gallagher – two of Britain's finest

When you were young and improving season by season, there was an argument for speeding up. Part of training is learning how hard you can push yourself, and this only comes from experience. You extend your limits and a time which was impossible last year becomes easy this year. Now we are mature runners, however, the law of diminishing returns sets in. We have to pick the session which is going to do us the most good, in relation to a particular target. If your 5 x 1 mile is aimed at racing in the 10k to 10 miles range, then it has got to be at 10k pace, a bit faster than threshold. You are accumulating blood lactate and your pulse rate is going up, if you tried to run them, say five seconds a mile faster, you would get a much higher lactate level, which could be damaging. You can cut down the recovery interval, using your pulse as a guide, this tells you that you are getting fitter, but probably does not have much effect on your performance. However, if you increase the distance run, say to 2000m or to a mile-and-a-half, and keep to the same pace or the same pulse rate, you will be training yourself to be more efficient and more enduring at that pace.

On the track it is easier, because you can easily add or subtract 200m or 400m to each rep. If your 5000m target is 17 minutes, then you need to get used

On the podium

to running 10–15 x 400m in 82 seconds. Your recovery time will start at say, a 200m jog in 2 minutes and then come down to 60 seconds flat. When it becomes easy to run 15 x 400m in that way, you should be mixing in 600s and 800s at that speed, with equal-time recovery. Your session might become 2 x 400m, 5 x 800m, 2 x 400m, all at 82 seconds a lap pace, with a fast lap at the end, or it might become 5 x (800+400m) and eventually 7 or 8 x 800m.

For a 10000m runner who regularly runs 6 x 800m on the track, the logical progression would be to move up to 8 x 800m and then start mixing in 1000m runs. The total distance of fast work should move up from six or seven thousand metres to over eight thousand, with the eventual target being the full ten thousand. In our experience, it is mentally easier to do a pyramid session. A session of 400-600-800-1000-1200-1000-800-600-400m adds up to 6800m but is more interesting than 6 x 1000m and therefore seems to go more quickly. You must be strict with your recovery times, however, if these sessions are to be compared with others.

The important thing is to remember what the session is for. If it is to increase your efficiency at race pace, then stay around race pace, with longer distances and shorter recoveries. If it is designed to prepare you for a hard race, then you have to get used to high blood lactate levels – running fast when tired. In this situation you would do 'speed endurance' sessions – fast runs over 1000–2000m, with long recoveries, say four to six minutes. However, we would only recommend one or two of these sessions in the last few weeks before your competitive peak. You should never lose sight of the fact that training is specific to races. Cultivate the skill of running efficiently at race pace.

A suitable schedule for a good veteran distance runner, aiming for times such as 3000m sub-9:30 (men) or sub 11:00 (women), 5000m sub-16:00 (men) or sub-18:00 (women) would be:

Week 1

Monday:	6 miles easy plus 6 x 150m stride-outs
Tuesday:	4 x 1200m or 5 x 1000m at 5000m pace, 3–4 mins rest between
Wednesday:	6 miles brisk run
Thursday:	4 x (800 + 400) at 3000m pace, 200m jog recovery
Friday:	Rest
Saturday:	3 x (4 x 400m) at 1500m pace, 60 secs recovery, with extra 3 mins recovery after each set
Sunday:	8–10 miles easy

Week 2

Monday:	3 x 2400m, off the track, at 10k pace, 5 mins recovery
Tuesday:	6–7 miles steady
Wednesday:	2 x (8 x 200m) at 1500m pace, 1 min recovery
Thursday:	4 miles easy run
Friday:	Rest or 20 mins jog
Saturday:	Race or: 10 mins hard, 5 mins recovery, 2 mins hard,5 mins recovery, 1 min hard – all on grass
Sunday:	8–10 miles easy

Allowances for age. Over-50: Only two hard sessions per week and allow one day for complete rest. Over-60: As for over-50, but reduce volume of hard sessions by one-third.

Variety in training

Steve Mottershead teaches and coaches at Millfield School. As a young man he trained very hard – 70 miles a week – but never reached more than good club standard as a distance runner. After turning 40 he changed to shorter distances, running less than 40 miles a week and doing more speed work. When he started to include weight training and gym work in his training, he noticed a marked improvement in performance, and at the age of 49 set a lifetime best of 54 secodns for 400 metres, more than 1 second faster than his previous best. Moreover, he can still run a respectable marathon. The moral of this is that you should always remain open-minded about trying new methods of making progress.

Steve James

age: **63** occupation: **retired IT manager**

When Bruce was a postgraduate at Cambridge in 1959, Steve James was an Oxford undergraduate – and a brilliant miler. In the annual Oxford-Cambridge cross-country match he beat me soundly. His career highlights go:

1959	National Junior cross-country champion
	Inter-Counties 3 miles champion
1993	World Veterans 10000m champion
	World record-holder for 5000m (over-55)
1995	World Veterans 10000m champion (over-55)
1998	World record-holder for 5000m (over-60)

After leaving Oxford, his professional career and family commitments restricted his running, so we shall never know what heights he might have reached, but his performances as a veteran suggest that he would have performed well at Olympic level. His British best of 33 mins 29 secs for 10k on the road, at the age of 60, was only one of many awesome performances.

Why do you like running? "Why do we like doing anything? Some of the things I like include being in a team, training in pleasant surroundings, travelling to interesting places and having targets to aim at. I enjoy it much more when the social side is good – the club is important.

"Running has been such a normal part of my life that I get itchy feet if I haven't been for a run for a day or two – my body seems to need it."

What motivates you to go on competing? "That is the best part!"

How do you fit in work, training and family? "The only answer has been to do less training than is required. In my first four years in industry we lived in five different houses. When we became more settled I did cross-country, on only 20–30 miles a week. In my Forties, having flexible working hours was a great help – now I'm retired, there is rarely a problem."

How has your approach changed, since reaching 40? "I did very little track running in my thirties and forties, so forty was not really a landmark. It meant two more cross-country races a year, but gradually the British Veterans cross-country became the main target of the year. At 52 I went to the World Vets in Eugene, Oregon, and I've been going to the World and European championships ever since. I still put in some hard training sessions, but I can't do as many in a week without getting over-tired."

F162

CHAPTER NINE

Racing 10k on the road

This is the most popular racing distance, but of course the schedules would work equally well for running any distance from 5k to 12k (three to eight miles). If you have been following the 'full fitness' programme you will be able to cope with a 10k race, but you won't have reached your full potential. This chapter really takes over from where Chapter 7 leaves off.

In the 'full fitness' programme we are recommending running four times a week, totalling about 22 miles (35 km) a week. A 50% increase in volume, running six times a week for a total of 33–35 miles, can easily be fitted in with the working week and will enable one to run close to one's best for distances of 8–10k (5–6 miles).

For the first few weeks, build up to 30 miles a week by increasing the number of sessions to five or six a week. Once your body can cope with this, bring in the quality sessions.

Bruce's basic 10k schedule

Week 1	
Monday:	Rest or 3 miles easy
Tuesday:	6 miles steady pace
Wednesday:	1 mile slow, then 30 minutes of Fartlek, running 30 secs, 1 min and 2 mins fast, with equal time jogging recoveries + 5 mins easy jog at end
Thursday:	5 miles easy, off road
Friday:	4–5 miles easy run before breakfast
Saturday:	Warm up, 10 x 400m on track (1 min rest), warm down
Sunday:	6–8 miles easy, off road

Week 2

Monday:	Rest
Tuesday:	5–6 miles steady run
Wednesday:	Warm up, 4 x 1000m on road (2 mins rest), warm down
Thursday:	5 miles easy, off road
Friday:	Rest or 4 miles easy
Saturday:	3 miles easy, with 6 x 100m fast stride
Sunday:	Warm up, RACE (8–10k) or 5k time trial, warm down

Age allowances. Over-55: aim for only one hard session a week, plus one long run, but have one rest day and one non-running day, e.g. cycling, swimming or gym work.

'Serious' 10000m schedule

The following schedule is a step up on the one above. It has a sufficiently large endurance element to cope with races from five miles up to ten miles.

Week 1

Monday:	6 mile steady run, with 6 x 100m strides at the end
Tuesday:	6 mile Fartlek, with 10 x 200m fast, last mile easy
Wednesday:	6 mile easy, off road if possible
Thursday:	5 mile Fartlek on hills, bursts up the hills
Friday:	Rest
Saturday:	Warm up, 3 x 1 mile brisk pace, (5 mins rest), warm down
Sunday:	8–10 mile slow run
Week's total:	36–38 miles

Week 2

Monday:	6–7 miles steady pace
Tuesday:	Warm up, 16 x 200m fast, 45 secs recovery
Wednesday:	5-6 miles easy
Thursday:	Run to hill, 8-10 x 45 secs uphill fast, run back
Friday:	Rest
Saturday:	Warm up, 3 mile timed run, warm down
Sunday:	8–10 miles easy pace
Week's Total:	36–40 miles

Mike Hager in the European Vets 10k, Malta 2001

Week 3

Monday:	6 miles steady pace
Tuesday:	15 x 400m fast 90 secs interval
Wednesday:	5 miles easy, off-road
Thursday:	6 miles Fartlek, on hills
Friday:	Rest
Saturday:	4 x 2000m repetition run, 5 mins recovery
Sunday:	12 miles slow run
Week's total:	45 miles approx

Week 4

Monday:	6 miles, steady pace
Tueday:	7 miles Fartlek
Wednesday:	5 miles easy, off-road
Thursday:	4 miles brisk pace, with bursts on hills, 1–2 miles easy at end
Friday:	Rest or 3 miles jog
Saturday:	30 mins easy, with a few strides
Sunday:	Race, 8–10 miles
Week's total:	40–45 miles approx

Week 5

Monday:	am: 4 mile jog – pm: 6 miles steady
Tuesday:	6 x 800m fast, + 4 x 400m (equal time recovery)
Wednesday:	5 miles easy
Thursday:	Hill running, 12 x 45 secs
Friday:	Rest or 3 miles jog
Saturday:	Warm up, 10 mins fast, 6 mins rest, 5 mins fast
Sunday:	10 miles steady run
Week's total:	45–48 miles approx

Week 6

Monday:	6 miles, start slowly, finish fast
Tuesday:	5 miles easy, off-road
Wednesday:	5 x 1 mile repetition run (4 mins rest)
Thursday:	7 miles slow run
Friday:	Rest or 3 miles jog
Saturday:	5 miles easy Fartlek
Sunday:	Minor race, 3–8 miles
Week's total:	40–45 miles

Week 7

Monday:	am: 5 miles jog pm: 6–7 miles steady pace
Tuesday:	7–8 miles good pace
Wednesday:	5 miles easy, off-road
Thursday:	Hill running, 12–14 x 45 secs
Friday:	4 miles jog
Saturday:	20 mins hard run, plus warm-up and cool down
Sunday:	12–14 miles slowly
Week's total:	50 miles approx

Week 8 (pre-race special week)

Monday:	7 miles steady, with 8 x 1 min fast, 1 min slow
Tuesday:	6 miles easy, off-road
Wednesday:	10 mins fast, 5 mins jog, 5 mins fast, 3 mins jog, 2 mins fast, warm down
Thursday:	4 miles jog
Friday:	6 miles easy, with strides
Saturday:	3 miles jog or rest
Sunday:	10K RACE
Week's total:	40 miles approx

Allowances for age. Over-50: not more than 2 hard runs per week, allow one day complete rest. Over-60: Not more than one hard run per week, allow one day for rest and one day for non-running activities.

Further progress

The perennial problem for the older runner is whether he should train harder to offset the inevitable slowing down or whether he should bow to the inevitable and not push himself so hard. There is no answer which will fit all cases. It is firstly a question of whether you have the time and the inclination to put in more training and secondly a question of what your body will stand.

The yearly programme

Take it season by season, spring, summer, autumn, winter.

As the days get longer, you can increase the total volume of training in March and April, and as it gets warmer you can start doing more fast sessions in April/May. With long summer days you may find that you can get out early and run for an hour before work, or run twice a day if you are retired – but only if you really want to, and if you can take it. August is a time when a lot of people are abroad on holiday, so you may cut your training back to running for half an hour every other day and then build up the miles again in September/October, when the weather is often very good for running. As Christmas approaches and the weather gets worse you have plenty of good reasons for going back into 'maintenance' mode, perhaps running three times a week and going to the gym for some weight training twice a week.

BRUCE: "At the end of each year I tot up my miles and look back on my racing results, and make fresh plans. When I know I am going to have the opportunity to train hard I schedule a couple of races for perhaps a month later, so that I have more incentive to keep the training going and enough time to get the benefit from it. When I know that I am going to be too busy to do much, I set a lower limit and say: I must run at least three times a week to stay reasonably fit, but I won't race until I have four weeks decent training behind me."

Expecting to be in top racing shape all the year round is bound to lead to disappointment, but if you come back to racing after a break you get all the more pleasure from the freshness of the experience.

A role model

Bill Foster on the road

In the picture to the right, Bill Foster is coming second in the World Veterans 10k Road Race, 2000. We can remember Bill running well in a schools 1500m when he was 16, and since then he has managed to combine a career as a geneticist with becoming a top class runner, a 2 hr 15 marathon runner, a British international in the European championships and the World Cup and a stalwart of Blackheath Harriers. As a veteran, he has cut down his training from the 100-miles-a-week of the international to a 'mere' 70 a week, which includes one hard interval session and one 'tempo' session – a sustained fast run over 6–7 miles.

He succeeds as a world-class veteran because he combines hard work with common sense; he looks after himself carefully, swims more, takes it easy after hard sessions and doesn't over-race. "I still enjoy competing for my club and I enjoy the relaxed atmosphere of Veterans competitions. I've had a fantastic time, travelling to lots of countries, and most of my friends are people I've met through running. I can't imagine life without it."

Road racing tactics and strategy

After the race we are all friends, sharing the same experience, but during it, the rivalry can become quite intense. Some men will run themselves into the ground rather than get beaten by a woman, while others, realising that the woman is competing in a different category, are helpful and encouraging, sharing the pacemaking.

The older you get, the more you need to use your head. With more experience, you should be better at pace judgement and also better at choosing the right clothing for each race. If you line up for a 10k race and see someone carrying a heavy water-bottle strapped to his backside, or see someone wearing long woolly tights in a ten-mile race, when they are bound to heat up, you know that there is someone putting themselves at a disadvantage.

Where you can really score is in getting the pace right from the start. If it's a 10k race and you are out to break 40 minutes, the right pace for the first kilometre is 3:55, or maybe slower if you have been held up at the start. My experience is that even pace or negative splits (second half of the race faster than the first) is the best policy, and if you do that you find yourself overtaking all the people of your ability who got it wrong in the first half.

The strategy lies in choosing your races during the year and over the years. A significant birthday, when you move up into a new five-year age-band, is often a good reason to launch a racing campaign, and likewise you will tend to race less when you are at the upper end (see Chapter 1).

Some people find that as they get older all they have left is endurance, so they run longer and longer races, or switch to multi-terrain and oddball events, where they can escape the tyranny of the watch. Others, like Steve Mottershead, find that with the right training they can do much better, relatively, in the shorter events, or they live somewhere where they can race indoors in the winter, so will adapt accordingly.

Battersea Park 5 miles

Predicting times

When you are moving up to race a longer distance for the first time, you can make a fairly a fairly accurate prediction of what you might do, on the basis of your times over 5k and 10k, as long as you have done the necessary training. Our guidelines are shown in Table 5 below.

Table 5: Equivalent performances

5k	10k	half marathon	Marathon
15:00	31:00	68:30	2 hr 27
16:00	33:15	73:30	2 hr 37
17:00	35:20	78:00	2 hr 48
18:00	37:25	83:00	2 hr 58
19:00	39:30	87:30	3 hr 07
20:00	41:35	92:00	3 hr 18
21:00	43:40	96:30	3 hr 27
22:00	45:45	1 hr 41	3 hr 37
23:00	47:50	1 hr 46	3 hr 48
24:00	49:55	1 hr 50	3 hr 58
25:00	52:00	1 hr 55	4 hr 08
30:00	63:00	2 hr 18	4 hr 58

Gareth Jones

age: **54** occupation: **Professor of Mathematics, Southampton University**

"I started running in my late thirties, because I felt I was becoming unfit: I was playing badminton and tennis regularly, but tiring towards the end of matches. Being competitive, I started entering road races to give myself a target, and when I ran 88 minutes for a hilly half marathon, in my second race, I realised that I had some ability. I soon dropped other sports and concentrated on running: I was soon winning vets prizes and by about 42 I was picking up BVAF medals. Between 42 and 47 I ran seven marathons, with a PB of 2 hr 26:57 in London, aged 43. I continued improving up to five years ago, when I ran my PB of 31:56 for 10k just before turning 49.

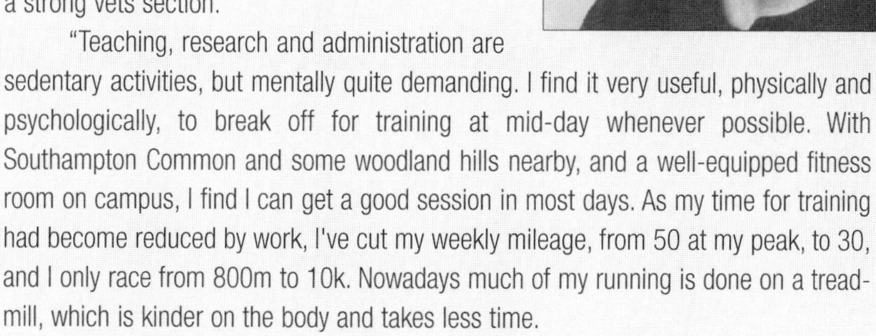

"Since then the ageing process, together with breaks due to asthma and sciatica, have caused a steady decline. My main motivation now is to complete for my club, Oxford City, which has a strong vets section.

"Teaching, research and administration are sedentary activities, but mentally quite demanding. I find it very useful, physically and psychologically, to break off for training at mid-day whenever possible. With Southampton Common and some woodland hills nearby, and a well-equipped fitness room on campus, I find I can get a good session in most days. As my time for training had become reduced by work, I've cut my weekly mileage, from 50 at my peak, to 30, and I only race from 800m to 10k. Nowadays much of my running is done on a treadmill, which is kinder on the body and takes less time.

"Athletics has brought me friendships with a much wider social range than university life and has taken me to places I wouldn't have dreamed of visiting. My mathematical research takes me all over the world, so I have been able to train in some challenging environments – in Kowloon, in the Negev desert and along the Olympic marathon courses in Atlanta and Moscow. The blue line is still there if you know where to look.

"My family and colleagues initially took a strong interest in my running (partly motivated by my being up with the leading women in televised road races), but familiarity converted enthusiasm into tolerance. Running is gradually losing ground in my list of priorities, but as long as I stay healthy I try to find time for it each day."

CHAPTER TEN

From ten miles to the half marathon

It's a challenge. You can say that of any distance, but it applies particularly to the half marathon. The full marathon is more than a challenge – it is a mountain to be climbed – but the fascination of the half is that while it is long enough to be impressive it is something which one can train for within the constraints of normal life. At twenty-one kilometres it demands considerable endurance. The normal thirty miles a week just isn't enough to cope properly with this distance.

To produce the best you are capable of you have got to be running at least fifty miles a week. At the highest level, of course, they are running one hundred miles a week or more,but this is for men who are running under 65 minutes and women under seventy-one minutes. At the same time, it is closer in speed to that of a 10k than to a marathon. In the middle stages of a 10k you are running only slightly faster than 'threshold' pace. This is the speed at which you start to accumulate lactic acid and as you get fitter you will be able to push back the threshold. In a ten-mile race you are running almost the whole distance at threshold, and if you are fit enough you can run the whole of your half marathon at 'threshold', too.

BRUCE: "You often find that in a good half marathon race you go through ten miles in close to your PB. I remember that when I was going for the over-sixty records in the spring of '96, I ran 58 minutes in the Woking Ten and a few weeks later ran 76:12 for the Bath half marathon, going through ten miles in a faster time than I had run at Woking. It follows from this that you should do the same training for a ten-mile race as for a half marathon."

For the schedules below we have set out three levels of training. The speed you run depends partly on your age and natural ability and partly on the amount of training you are doing.

Level One: This is for beginners and for those who have run the distance once or twice before, around the two-hour mark. It is also the right level for the over-fifties (all except the really keen ones). The principle is one of regular running with a gradual increase in distance. The most important run is the long one at weekends,but it will make a lot of difference if you put in the faster bits indicated during the week, rather than just plodding.

Level Two: This is much more demanding, working up to nearly five hours of training a week (or about forty miles), with two or three 'quality' sessions a week. This would be a reasonable training load for men hoping to run in the 1 hr 20 to 1 hr 30 range, or women hoping for 1 hr 25 to 1 hr 40. Over-forty runners moving up from 10k should start at this level unless they are already running under 37 minutes for 10k (men) or under 40 minutes (women).

Level Three: This goes up to fifty miles a week, or about six hours a week. Although this is only an hour or so more than Level Two, it does represent a considerable increase in effort, because there is more fast work. The Level Three person will be running much further in his forty minutes than those at Levels One and Two. There is more emphasis on continuous fast-paced runs, because you need to build up your 'speed-endurance' for a half marathon. The pace of these will be close to threshold which is the speed you will be running at for most of the race.

Distribution of effort

The pattern of 'hard-easy-hard-easy' is obvious in these schedules.Very often runners fall into 'one-pace' training, where that pace is not fast enough to give much of a training effect.

Running for 35–40 minutes a day will certainly make you fit enough to run a half marathon but your speed won't improve unless you are working at something approaching 'threshold' pace or faster. Endurance is built up both by the accumulation of the total distance run and by the distance of the longer runs. Until you are very experienced you should not be trying to run fast in the endurance runs.

The half marathon is run at threshold pace

Making progress

Whichever level you are on, you should be feeling much fitter after your first month. The person who manages to follow the schedule to the letter is very rare, but as long as you have done most of the training you will be ready for the next upward step. You will not be running greater distances. The key is running faster in the hard sessions. The more you train, the more you learn about your body and the better you are able to push yourself. Sometimes it is mentally easier to run round a five or six mile circuit fast than it is to run slowly, because when you run fast you are concentrating hard on the running and not worrying about how far you have to go.

Level One

Now that we have reached a 'plateau' of fitness, you will be able to cope with one 'quality' day when you are pushing yourself harder. The term 'fast' means the fastest speed that you can keep up for that length of time. As the recovery time is quite short, you will soon discover how fast you can afford to run and as time goes on you will find that this increased pace translates itself into improved times.

Level Two

Because the Level Two people are more experienced and faster runners, 35 minutes running may well be over five miles for them, whereas it will be only four miles for those on Level One. It is a good idea to time yourself over an exactly measured distance every two or three weeks. These schedules have timed sections in them, such as the repetition miles, which will give you something by which to measure your improvement, and each time you come back to them you can push yourself a little harder.

Level Three

The work load is much heavier here, as there are fewer days which are purely recuperative. Although the total distance covered is not huge – five hours represents only about 45 miles – it is still a pretty strenuous programme if done properly.

Note that Week 7 has much less in it. The occasional easy week can be put in either to let you recover, if you find that you are getting more and more tired, or simply in order for you to be fresh for the race.

Making the effort

On paper, 40 minutes of easy running might look like more than 30 minutes of hard running, so it is important to give an idea of how hard you have run. I suggest that you record your effort level in your training diary, on a scale of 1 to 10.

1	Minimal jog
2 – 3	Easy running, 50% effort or less
4 – 5	Steady running – this is slower than race pace but more than just a jog. If the weather is bad or the route long and hilly, it could reach 6
6 – 7	Brisk running and Fartlek. Stretches of this will be at your race pace, which is the same as your threshold pace, and in the Fartlek some bits will be even faster
8 – 9	Hard training, interval and repetition sessions
10	Race or flat-out time-trial effort

Recording the total time run and the number of 'effort points' in the week will give you a good idea of how hard you are training.

Level One programme (four days a week)

Week 1	
Day 1:	25 mins easy
Day 2:	25 mins easy
Day 3:	35 mins easy
Day 4:	25 mins brisk timed run

Week 2	
Day 1:	25 mins easy
Day 2:	30 mins easy, with a few 50m bursts
Day 3:	30 mins easy
Day 4:	45–50 mins

Week 3	
Day 1:	35 mins easy
Day 2:	35 mins easy, with a few 100m bursts
Day 3:	10 mins warm-up, 20 mins timed run, 5 mins jog
Day 4:	50–60 mins steady run

Week 4	
Day 1:	35 mins easy
Day 2:	35 mins easy, including several 30-second bursts
Day 3:	35 mins steady
Day 4:	60 mins steady run

Week 5	
Day 1:	35 mins easy
Day 2:	40–45 mins of fast-and-slow running, doing bursts uphill
Day 3:	35 mins easy
Day 4:	Warm-up, 10k race, warm down, or 65–70 mins steady run

Week 6	
Day 1:	30mins easy, off road if possible
Day 2:	10 mins warm-up, then 2 x 5 mins fast, 5 mins jog
Day 3:	35 mins easy
Day 4:	65–70 mins steady run

Zina Marchant – a great half marathon performer

Week 7

Day 1:	30–35 mins easy, off road.
Day 2:	30 mins run, including 10 fast bursts of about 200m
Day 3:	30 mins easy
Day 4:	Warm-up, 10k race, 10 mins walking and jogging

Week 8

Day 1:	35–40 mins easy, off road
Day 2:	35 mins jog, 20 mins brisk pace, 5 mins jog
Day 3:	30 mins easy
Day 4:	80–90 mins slow run (this is your longest!)

Week 9

Day 1:	30 mins easy, off road
Day 2:	10 mins jog, 2 x 5 mins fast (as Week 6)
Day 3:	30 mins easy
Day 4:	60–70 mins easy pace

Week Ten

Day 1:	20 mins jog
Day 2:	10 mins jog, 1 mile at race pace, in racing shoes, 10 mins jog
Day 3:	20 mins jog, in racing kit
Day 4:	RACE

Level Two programme (5–6 days a week)

Week 1

Monday:	35–40 mins easy
Tuesday:	35 mins, faster than Monday
Wednesday:	40 mins, including 10 x 30 secs fast, 60 secs slow
Thursday:	35 mins easy
Friday:	Rest
Saturday:	40 mins steady, with several 100m strides
Sunday:	50–60 mins easy

Week 2

Monday:	35 mins easy
Tuesday:	40–45 mins steady, faster up hills.
Wednesday:	40 mins steady, including 8 x (1 min fast, 1 min slow)
Thursday:	40 mins easy
Friday:	Rest
Saturday:	Warm-up, 3 miles (approx) timed run, warm-down
Sunday:	60 mins steady run

Week 3

Monday:	35 mins easy
Tueday:	40–45 mins, starting slow, finishing fast
Wednesday:	35 mins easy
Thursday:	10 mins easy, 8 x (90 secs fast, 90 secs slow), 5 mins easy
Friday:	Rest
Saturday:	10–15 mins warm-up, 4 x 800m (or 3 mins) fast, with 3 mins slow recovery jog
Sunday:	65 mins steady run

Week 4

Monday:	35 mins easy
Tuesday:	40 mins brisk pace
Wednesday:	Warm-up, 3 x 1 mile fast (or 3 x 6 mins), 3 mins recovery jog, 5 mins warm-down
Thursday:	35 mins easy
Friday:	Rest
Saturday:	Warm-up, 10k race or time trial over 5 miles.
Sunday:	65–70 mins steady run

Week 5

Monday:	35 mins easy
Tuesday:	40 mins, starting steadily, finishing fast
Wednesday:	As last Wednesday, but do 4 repetitions, not 3
Thursday:	35 mins easy, with 6 x 150 metres fast stride
Friday:	Rest or 20 mins jog
Saturday:	10 mins easy, 10 mins brisk pace, 10 mins easy
Sunday:	Warm-up, 10k race or 6 miles at half marathon pace

Week 6

Monday:	35 mins easy, off road
Tuesday:	5 mins easy, 15 x 1 min fast, 1 min slow, 5 mins jog
Wednesday:	10 mins steady, 2 x 10 mins at threshold pace (5 mins recovery jog)
Thursday:	40 mins steady
Friday:	Rest or 20 mins jog
Saturday:	10 mins warm-up, 20 mins hard run, 10 mins jog
Sunday:	70 mins steady run, off road

Week 7

Monday:	35 mins easy
Tuesday:	Rest
Wednesday:	50–55 mins run at a good pace
Thursday:	35–40 mins easy, with 10 x 100m stride
Friday:	Rest
Saturday:	30 mins off road, with 6 x 30 secs stride
Sunday:	Warm-up, Race, 6- 10 miles,10 mins walk-jog

Week 8

Monday:	35–40 mins easy
Tuesday:	40 mins Fartlek on hilly course, with bursts up hills
Wednesday:	Warm-up, 4 x 1 mile as Week 5, but faster
Thursday:	35 mins steady
Friday:	Rest or 20 mins jog
Saturday:	10 mins steady, then 15 x 40 secs fast, 50 secs jog, 5–10 mins steady at the end
Sunday:	75–85 mins steady endurance run

Week 9

Monday:	35 mins easy,off road
Tuesday:	40 mins, including 8 x 2mins fast, 1 min slow
Wednesday:	Warm-up, 2 x 2 miles threshold, as Week 6, but faster
Thursday:	35–40mins steady
Friday:	Rest
Saturday:	Warm-up, three miles fast, timed,10 mins jog
Sunday:	60 mins steady

Week 10

Monday:	20 mins easy, off road
Tuesday:	Warm up, 2 x 1 mile at race pace, 5 mins jog recovery, warm down
Wednesday:	Rest or 20 mins easy jog
Thursday:	10 mins jogs, 6 x (30 secs fast, 60 secs slow), 15 mins jog
Friday:	Rest
Saturday:	20 mins jog
Sunday:	The Race

Level Three programme (6–7 days a week)

Week 1

Monday:	35 mins easy
Tuesday:	45 mins steady run
Wednesday:	Warm-up, 4 x 1200m (or 4 x 4 mins) with 3 min recovery jog, warm-down
Thursday:	40 mins easy
Friday:	Rest or 20 mins jog
Saturday:	40–50 mins steady run, with a few surges
Sunday:	70 mins slow run

Week 2

Monday:	35 mins easy
Tuesday:	45 mins hilly run, with bursts up hills
Wednesday:	35 mins easy
Thursday:	40 mins brisk run, including 10 x 1 min fast, 1 min slow
Friday:	Rest or 20 mins jog
Saturday:	10 mins jog, 30 mins brisk pace, 5 mins jog
Sunday:	65–70 mins steady run

Week 3

Monday:	40 mins easy
Tuesday:	5 mins easy, 30–35 mins brisk run, 5 mins easy
Wednesday:	Warm-up, 4 x 1 mile (or 4 x 5 mins), 4 min recoveries
Thursday:	35 mins easy
Friday:	Rest or 20 mins jog
Saturday:	50–55 mins Fartlek, with long fast bursts
Sunday:	70–75 mins slow run

Week 4

Monday:	40 mins easy
Tuesday:	Fast hilly run as Week 2
Wednesday:	40 mins easy
Thursday:	10 mins easy, 2 x 2 mins fast, 2 mins slow, 4 x (1 min fast, 1 min slow), 8 x (30 secs fast, 1 min slow), 5 mins jog
Friday:	Rest or 20 mins jog
Saturday:	Warm-up, Race 10k or 6 miles fast timed run
Sunday:	70–80 mins slow run

Week 5

Monday:	40–45 mins easy
Tuesday:	10 mins steady, 6 x 2 mins fast, 2 mins slow
Wednesday:	40 mins steady run
Thursday:	Warm-up, 12 x 400m, 90 secs recovery or 15 x 1 min fast, 1 min slow, warm-down
Friday:	Rest or 20 mins jog
Saturday:	Warm-up, 5 miles fast, 10 mins jog, or 30 mins easy if racing on Sunday
Sunday:	Warm-up, race 6–10 miles, warm down, or 75 mins steady endurance run

Week 6

Monday:	40 mins easy, off road
Tuesday:	10 mins easy, 3 x 2 miles at threshold pace, 6 min recovery
Wednesday:	35–40 mins easy
Thursday:	45 mins Fartlek, off road if possible, including 15–20 fast bursts of 150–200m
Friday:	20 mins slow jog
Saturday:	30 mins easy run
Sunday:	20 mins warm-up, low-key race, long warm-down or 90 mins slow endurance run

Week 7

Monday:	35 mins easy, off road
Tuesday:	Rest
Wednesday:	15 mins easy, 5 miles at race pace, 10 mins jog
Thursday:	35 mins off road, including 8 x 200m fast stride
Friday:	Rest or 30 mins jog

Saturday:	Rest
Sunday:	Warm up, Race, 6–10 miles, warm down

Week 8

Monday:	40 mins very slowly
Tuesday:	50–55 mins Fartlek on hilly course,bursts up hills
Wednesday:	40 mins steady
Thursday:	Warm up, 5 x 1 mile, timed, 3 mins recovery
Friday:	20 mins easy
Saturday:	35–40 mins on grass, with 8 x 200m stride
Sunday:	Endurance run, 1 hr 30–1 hr 45

Week 9

Monday:	40 mins easy, off road
Tuesday:	Warm up, 3 x 2 miles, as Week 6
Wednesday:	40 mins easy
Thursday:	Warm-up, 2 sets of 4 x 1 min fast, 1 min slow, with 5 mins jog between sets
Friday:	20 mins jog
Saturday:	Warm up, 20 mins at race pace, 5 mins jog
Sunday:	60 mins steady, no pressure

Week Ten

Monday:	30 mins easy, off road
Tuesday:	Warm up, 2 miles at race pace, 2 mile jog
Wednesday:	Rest or 20 mins jog
Thursday:	10 mins jog, 10 x 30 secs fast, 1 min slow, 5 mins warm down
Friday:	Rest
Saturday:	20 mins jog, in racing kit, with easy strides
Sunday:	The Race

The final stage

In the last stages of a training programme there is not much you can do to make yourself run faster. Putting in hard training at this stage is counterproductive because there is not time for the body to respond to the stresses you are imposing on it, and if you are not fully recovered you will be tired when you start. On the other hand, if you did no training at all in the last two weeks, you would start to lose fitness. You need to do enough to maintain aerobic fitness, maintain your

The Lake Vyrnwy Half marathon is a very popular event

endurance and keep your weight down. Maintaining aerobic fitness is best done by doing short brisk sessions at threshold pace or faster. This is why we recommend sessions like 10 x 30 secs fast, or 2 miles at race speed. General endurance is maintained by a weekly run of at least an hour, plus the regular outings during the week.

The reason why training is reduced in the last few days – the tapering period – is so that the muscle glycogen stores have a chance to build up again and damaged muscle cells are either repaired or replaced. Because your body is used to running regularly, it is better to go out and do a twenty-minute session rather than rest. This also gives you a chance to try out the running kit, particularly the shoes and socks, which you will be wearing in the race. If you have got new shoes for the race, or if your old ones have just packed up on you, make sure that the new ones are broken in. Wear them several times before you race in them, and do at least one good session at race pace.

Warning signs

If you have a muscle strain, or an infection, such as a bad cold or a touch of 'flu', in the week of the race – don't run. It is not worth taking the risk. Enter another race three or four weeks later, giving yourself a chance to rest up, then put in one or two weeks of normal training before tapering off again.

Targets

Getting the pace right at the start makes a huge difference in a long race. If in doubt, err on the side of caution. In relation to your 10k pace, your half marathon pace is going to be three to ten seconds a kilometre slower. There is also the extra

1.1 kilometres to be taken into account. As a rough guide, the person who runs a 10k in 37 minutes should add on 60 seconds and double it to get an estimate of the time at 20k, then add on the time taken for the extra 1.1 km, e.g.

38:00 x 2 = 76 mins for 20k + 5 mins = 81 mins for 21.1k

The person who runs 45 mins for 10k should get:

46:30 x 2 = 93:00 for 20k, + 8 mins = 99:00

for the half marathon (see also Chapter 9, p. 116).

Having established a target time, we would suggest running the first three miles as close to that speed as possible. If you are really fit, and finding this pace comfortable, it is possible to pick up the pace by a few second per mile and get well inside your target time, but if you are lacking in endurance, starting at this speed, rather than going off fast, will give you a better chance of finishing in a respectable time. The speed will feel comfortable in the early stages, but give yourself three miles at that pace before you make any decisions.

Tactics

For most of us, the best tactics are just running at a level pace, in the appropriate section of the field, and trying to use our fellow-competitors as pacemakers. If you go off at level pace it is very encouraging when you find that you are pulling back those who started faster, whereas if you go off too fast and slow down, it is very discouraging to be caught and passed in the second half of the race. If you are up at the sharp end it is a different matter.

As there are so many half marathons run nowadays, it is quite common for races to be won in over 70 minutes, and of course age-group times may be correspondingly slow as well. A good veteran runner may find him or herself in with a chance of a win. Nigel Gates was still winning open races at the age of 47.

In this case it is worth deviating from level pace in order to get an advantage. If you are a lady hoping to run 78 mins something – 6 minute mile pace – and you have a rival whose best time is, say, 79 minutes, it is better to go off with men who are running 76–77-minute pace. They can set the pace for you and maybe protect you from the wind, whereas if you were running at 78:30 pace from the start, your rival could run with you and take advantage of your pacemaking.

Last thoughts

On the morning of the race, eat your last meal, something simple and digestible, three hours beforehand. In the twenty-four hours before that, lay off high-fibre foods, because they may serious consequences during the race! Keep on taking drinks, if it is hot, up to thirty minutes beforehand, and if necessary, drink more just before the start, so that the fluid does not have time to be taken up by your kidneys. For an autumn race, go prepared for all weathers, from singlet and lightweight shorts, to tights, gloves and woolly hat – and plenty of rain gear to keep you dry before and after the race.

Margaret Auerback

age: **53** occupation: **artist**

Margaret Auerback started running at the age of 33, to lose weight. Twenty years later, she has lost weight but she is still running. Like so many, she started by wanting to run a marathon but got injured and had to stop. She ran her first marathon in 1982 and it was a bit of a disaster – "OK for twenty miles and pretty grim for the last six". Unlike most others, though, she persevered and knocked thirty-five minutes off her time in the next one, running 3 hr 13 minutes. She joined her local running club, Ranelagh Harriers, quite early in her running career and says that this has done a lot to keep her in the sport. They have fixtures all the year round, in track, cross-country and road running, which gives her something to train for.

Margaret's biggest successes, though, have come from veteran running, and all her best times have been set since she passed her 40th birthday. At the age of 40 she ran 2 hr 48 for a marathon (a time which would please most 40-year-old men) and also gained her first international recognition, after finishing 2nd in the National Vets cross-country.

Since turning 50 she has been consistently successful, winning the national over fifty cross-country title and running for England for three successive years in the cross-country international. In the 1997 London marathon, she was the first over-fifty woman, running the distance in 3 hr 3 mins.

"The reason I am still running is above all because I enjoy it. I run with friends maybe twice a week and at the weekend I do a long run with my husband. Over the years running has enabled us to explore a lot of different places, in Crete, in Kenya, in Portugal and in France.

"I think what motivates me most is training for a particular event, such as selection for a vets international. I have that date in my mind and every session is part of my plan. I know that I can't improve on the PBs I set years ago, so now I have different aims, either PBs in a new age group, or trying different events. For example, I want to try more long distance events and more mountain events – not easy in Richmond! I will continue running for my club in league races.

"Over the years my training has changed little, but I seldom train twice a day now, and I sometimes replace an easy run with cycling to lessen the jarring on the legs. I run 40–50 miles a week, I try to do two gym sessions a week and I am planning to improve my swimming. No, I don't plan to do a triathlon – a duathlon perhaps?"

FLORA
1 MILE

CHAPTER ELEVEN

The Marathon

Can you take up marathon running when you are over forty? Definitely. There are hundreds of examples, of which Richard Cashmore (p. 162) is just one. Older runners have more endurance and greater mental strength than younger runners – but they need to be more careful about their training.

Some of us come to the marathon after years of running shorter distances. It is something which you do when you are losing some of your speed, because speed is much less important here than endurance. Almost every distance runner has the ambition to run a marathon before they retire. Sometimes the results are startling. There was a club runner in Essex, called Ian Thompson, who was asked in 1974 to make up the club team for the AAA marathon championships. He was a goodish 10k and cross-country runner, well below international standard – but he turned out to be a natural marathon runner. He won the first marathon of his life in 2 hr 12 minutes and went on to become the European and Commonwealth champion in the same year. Something in his internal chemistry made him a much better marathon runner than anyone suspected, but if he hadn't been asked to run he might not have found out.

For some runners, the marathon is the only race. The reason they take up running is to run a marathon, because they have seen it on television and they want to find out whether they can do it. It is hard, and the reason that it is hard is that the normal human body only stores enough carbohydrate to last us for 15–20 miles of hard running. Walking twenty-six miles is not a problem, because when we are walking we are only burning up 400 calories an hour and we can use our fat reserves – and of course we can take more fuel on board while we are walking. When you are running fast, in-flight refuelling is not impossible, but it is limited. We therefore have, as well as the problems of muscle fatigue and dehydration, the problem of running out of glucose, which we call 'hitting the wall'

At 22 miles in the London Marathon

and the faster you run, the more likely you are to hit it.

Even if you avoid the wall, the experience of racing forty-two kilometres is quite unlike anything you meet at shorter distances.

In different marathons we have gone through the full range of emotional experience – the tedium of waiting for the day, the panic of getting to the start, the terror of anticipation, the joy of running really well, the shame of being reduced to a shambling wreck, love of one's fellow runners, hate for the idiot who says something stupid when you are tired, contentment and triumph, disappointment, envy and, finally, that erosion of the identity, a reduction of the personality to its basic level, which you otherwise meet only under the threat of death.

In a marathon, you find out who you are.

Even if you have run many marathons, the next one will not be the same as the last one, and for all of us it remains a big challenge, not to be taken lightly, the urban man's Everest.

The actual schedules run for fourteen weeks, which means that if you start after New Year your schedule will be right for London, Boston, Paris, Rotterdam or any other of the ten big events which take place in mid- or late April. By repeating a module of two or four weeks you can be in even better shape for a May marathon. Before that, however, you need to assess yourself.

The following questionnaire, which was used in *Running* magazine a few years ago, will give you some idea of where you stand – but it is only a rough idea.

Are you fit to run a marathon?

1.	**You are prepared to have a go**	+10 points
2.	**Your age**	
	18–19	0
	20–35	+5
	36–40	+3
	41–48	0
	49–55	–1
	56–61	–3
	62–69	–5
3.	**Smoking habits**	
	non-smoker	+5
	'occasional' or 'social' smoker	0
	5–20 cigs/week	–5
	21–40 cigs/week	–10
	subtract 5 points for every additional 20 cigs/week	
4.	**Drinking habits**	
	(one unit is a small glass of wine or half a pint of beer)	
	non-drinker	0
	up to 7 units per week	0
	8–15 units per week	–5
	subtract one point for each additional unit	
5.	**Your weight**	
	definitely skinny	+5
	under average weight	+2
	about average	0
	slightly overweight	–10
	considerably overweight	–20
6.	**Your health**	
	'Never ill'	+2
	the 'occasional cold'	0
	frequent colds or coughs	–5

	ill in bed in the last two months	–10
	serious illness or injury in the last 3 months	–20
7.	**Exercise* habits**	
	(take your average for the last 4 weeks)	
	less than once a week	–5
	once a week	0
	twice a week	+5
	add two points for each additional day (max. score 15 points)	
	or miles walked per week	
	- *1–10 miles: +1 point per mile*	
	- *over 10 miles: +1/2 point per mile*	
	or miles run per week: +1 point per mile	

* 'Exercise' means 30 minutes of moderately strenuous exercise, such as aerobics, football, squash or cycling. Golf counts as walking.

So, Molly Meanswell, under 35, non-smoker, who exercises twice a week, will have 25 points. Joe Jogger, over 40, who runs 15 miles a week and is slightly below average weight, but is a 'social' smoker and drinker, will have 32 points. Mr. Slob, who took it on for a bet, is under 35, but smokes and drinks, takes no exercise and is overweight, will have minus 25.

To start the Get-You-Round programme you need 30 points. To start the sub-4 hr programme you need 40 points To start the sub-3 hr 30 programme you need 50 points. To start the sub-3 hr programme you need 60 points.

Even Mr. Slob could run a marathon – but he would have to cut out the booze and the fags, get into walking ten miles a week and bring his weight down to normal. In a couple of months he would be able to start regular jogging and have enough points to follow the GYR schedule.

Molly Meanswell would need an additional five points for the GYR programe, which she could easily gain by adding five miles a week of running and walking to her normal routine. If she were able to run a further ten miles a week she could start on the sub-4 hours schedule.

It's all in the mind, you know

There is one more thing you need – the marathon mindset. It is not just making a decision now, it is the commitment to keep it going for more than three months.

You have to schedule regular training into your lifestyle – find time, get running partners, find nice places to run. The long runs are much easier if you have someone to run with – and you are less likely to back out once you have committed yourself.

Age and the marathon

As you get older, you may lose speed, but your endurance depends on your training. If you are fit enough to run a 45-minute 10k, whatever your age, you can build up to running a half marathon in 100 minutes, and if you can do that, it is possible to build up to a 3 hr 30 marathon. It is just a matter of training. The things most likely to affect older runners are muscle pulls, which may be caused by running when stiff, running when cold, or trying to run too fast. All these things may be avoided by caution and thorough warming up. The older you get, the more attention you should pay to retaining your flexibility and your leg strength and incorporating this into the training.

A word of warning

Just because you are following the sub-4 hr programme it does not follow that you will achieve this goal. All we can do is help you to develop your potential. There are people who can waltz round in three hours on practically no training. Conversely, if you are built like a two-hundred-and twenty-pound brick shit-house, you would have to train incredibly hard to break four hours. All we can do is try.

Another word of warning

Training is supposed to improve your health. If you find yourself permanently tired and run-down, and getting coughs and colds, give yourself a couple of days off and think about setting yourself an easier target for this year.

The Hundred Day plan

The first Hundred Day plan was published in *Runner's World* about ten years ago, and has been slightly modifed over the years by readers' feedback. If you are thinking of running the London, Paris or Boston Marathons, your hundred days

Ten steps to success

To reinforce your commitment, we have put ten steps into each programme, to act as milestones. These are designed to give you reassurance that you are making progress, and also to give you an idea of what marathon time you can expect.

Step	Distance	Time: sub-4 hrs	sub-3 hrs 30	sub-3 hrs
1	3 miles	24:00	21:00	18:00
	5k	25:00	22:00	18:45
2	12 miles*	2 hr 00:00	1 hr 45:00	1 hr 30:00
3	5 miles	40:00	35:00	30:00
	10k	52:00	45:30	39:00
4	15 miles*	2 hr 40:00	2 hr 20:00	2 hr 00:00
5	10k	51:00	44:00	38:00
6	10 miles	1 hr 22:00	1 hr 12:00	1 hr 02:00
7	18 miles*	3 hr 00:00	2 hr 40:00	2 hr 15:00
8	10 miles	1 hr 20:00	1 hr 10:00	1 hr 00:00
	half marathon	1 hr 52:00	1 hr 38:00	1 hr 24:00
9	half marathon	1 hr 50:00	1 hr 36:00	sub-1 hr 23:00
10	20 miles*	3 hr 20:00	2 hr 55:00	2 hr 30:00

* training run, other times are for races

start in early or mid- January. If you are planning to run Boston, which is on a Monday, train as if it was on the Sunday and lose the day you spend flying to Boston, which will be during your tapering period.

If you decide to start your programme on January lst, you have time in hand. You can give yourself a packet of free days, to be used when you are either to busy to run, or don't feel like doing more than a short jog. This is fine, as long as you only take them one at a time.

Choosing your programme

The four levels of training are labelled according to your expected marathon time, but they also reflect your degree of commitment or time available. You can predict your marathon potential from Table 5 (p. 116). Thus, a young fit person might only have time to follow the sub-4 hr programme, but still run under three hours. Someone of less ability, who ran well over four hours last year, but who is prepared to give up the time, could well follow the sub-3 hr 30 schedule and improve by a greater amount.

Beginning Marathon training

Day 1 (all levels)

A testing run. We all have our regular courses, and we have an idea of how far they are. For your first step on the marathon road we want you to go out and run a course which takes you more than fifteen but not more than thirty minutes to get round. Run round it steadily and make a note of your time. This is a bench mark. Don't race it. It is better to start slowly and finish faster than the other way round.

Day 2

This doesn't have to be the day after Day 1 – you can allow yourself a couple of days rest if you are tired. This is your first endurance run. Don't worry about how fast or slow you are going, walk if you have to, but pick out a loop as long as anything you have done before, preferably traffic-free and preferably interesting. Although we are going to race on the road, it is best to train off-road, when possible, which means at weekends for most of us. We suggest 5–6 miles for the Get-You-Round brigade and at least 10 miles for the sub-3-hours people.

How to use the schedules

The first six weeks

It would be remarkable if you were able to do every day as the schedule says. Some days you will be too busy or too tired, some days the roads will be dangerous. The training at all levels builds up in both volume and intensity. If you are really tired from a race or a hard session you should just run easily until you feel ready to train hard again, regardless of the schedule. What you should do is pick out the key elements in the week's training and try to get those done, fitting in the easier days as best you can.

The long runs, becoming progressively longer, are the most vital elements, and you should try to get those in if nothing else. The hill running will build up your leg strength and the repetition, interval or Fartlek training will improve your aerobic fitness – they will improve your basic running speed.

Occasional timed runs round your set course should confirm this. If you record what you actually do alongside what you are supposed to be doing, you will be able to see whether you are keeping the various elements in balance, and recording your weekly mileage will give you a rough idea of whether you are doing enough in total.

Races are also important, as well as being fun. Running in a race can bring out things you didn't know you had in you (and we don't mean last night's curry) and in any case you need to learn how to handle long-distance races before you run your marathon. Things like eating before the race, drinking during the race, working out your pre-race routine, are best done by experience.

Weeks 7–12

This is the hardest part of the training. The first flush of enthusiasm has gone and you still have a long way to go. For this reason we suggest running races at regular intervals. Half-marathons are obviously good for getting into your racing rhythm. You should train through them, not making them flat-out efforts, but starting at marathon pace and speeding up later on if you feel good. That is what we recommend, but when when you start racing them it is difficult not to be competitive. You could try running 6 or 7 miles before starting the a half marathon, giving a twenty-mile run. This makes the long Sunday morning run a lot easier, but you need to get your timing right. Perhaps it might be better to run the half marathon first, with a 2-mile warm-up, and then to do a five-mile warm-down.

The Get-You-Round and sub-4 hr programmes

For the followers of these programmes, the problem is maintaining one's equilibrium. You are probably doing more training than ever before and after a long run or a repetition session you feel tired. There should be enough variety and enough rest in the programme to cope with this, but everyone reacts differently. What do you do when you really don't feel that you can cope with the next day's training ? You say: "I'll put my kit on and just jog for a mile." When you've done that, you may feel like going on and doing more, but if you don't, call that one of your rest days and stop. You may need one more day's rest before you are ready to carry on, in which case you can ignore the missed day, but if it develops into a whole week of feeling tired, you are obviously overdoing it. You should either cut down on the training load and sets your sights a little lower or give yourself more time to adjust and move your race date back a few weeks.

Ten steps for the Get-You-Round

tick when achieved

1	Run 2 miles non-stop	☐	7	Run a 10-mile race (but you can walk!)	☐
2	Run 3 miles	☐	8	Walk/jog 15 miles	☐
3	Walk/jog 10 miles	☐	9	Run a half marathon race	☐
4	Run a 3–5 mile race	☐	10	Walk/jog 18 miles or more	☐
5	Walk/jog 12 miles	☐			
6	Run a 10k race	☐			

The sub-3 hr and sub-3 hr 30 programmes

The runners following these programmes should have more self-knowledge than those less experienced. They can distinguish between the tiredness which always comes after a hard session and the deep fatigue which come from training too hard day after day. We recommend them to work hard on their quality sessions, because they will benefit from them, but to treat themselves gently on the in-between days.

Remember that it is the rest between the sessions that enables your body to adjust.

The Get-You-Round programme

Days 3-9	
3	Rest
4	20 mins jogging, with stops when needed
5	Rest
6	20 mins jogging – you are allowed to walk, but it doesn't count
7	Rest
8	25 mins jogging and walking
9	55–60 mins jogging and walking

Days 10-16	
10	Rest
11	20–25 mins jogging
12	Rest
13	20–25 mins jogging
14	Rest
15	25–30 mins jogging and walking
16	80–90 mins jogging and walking

Day 17-23	
17	Rest
18	20 mins jogging
19	Rest
20	25 mins jogging
21	Rest
22	25 mins jogging, no stops
23	As Day 16, but with less walking

Days 24-30	
24	Rest
25	25 mins jogging
26	Rest
27	Warm up, timed run round your course (15–30 mins)
28	Rest
29	1 mile easy, 15 mins brisk continuous run, 1 mile jog
30	75–80 mins, alternating 10 mins running, 3 mins walking

Days 31-37	
31	Rest
32	20–25 mins run, with a few faster bursts
33	Rest
34	15 mins fast continuous run as Day 29
35	Rest
36	20 mins easy jog
37	10k road race or 90 mins walk-jog

Days 38-44	
38	Rest
39	25–30 mins steady run
40	Rest
41	Warm up, then 8 x 30 secs uphill fast, jog back
42	Rest
43	25–30 mins steady
44	60 mins jogging, walking as little as possible

Days 45-51	
45	Rest
46	30 mins steady run
47	30 mins run, inc. 6 x lmin fast, 2 mins jog
48	5 mins jog,10-15 mins brisk run,5 mins jog
49	Rest
50	30 mins steady run
51	8 miles endurance run,walking when necessary

Days 52-58	
52	Rest
53	30 mins run, inc. 4 x 60 secs fast and 4 x 30 secs fast
54	Rest

Avoidance of injury should always be top of the list

55	Warm up, 2 miles timed run, 5 mins jog
56	Rest
57	20 mins easy run
58	Half marathon race or 12 miles endurance run

Days 59-65

59	Rest
60	30 mins steady run
61	Warm up, 2 x 1 mile, timed, with 5 mins rest
62	25 mins easy run
63	Rest
64	30 mins steady run, working harder up the hills
65	9–10 miles endurance run, walking when necessary

Days 66-72

66	Rest
67	25–30 mins easy run
68	Warm up, timed run over 3 miles
69	20 mins steady run
70	Rest
71	25–30 mins steady, less if racing next day
72	Half-marathon race, or two-hour run with friends

Days 73-79

73	Rest
74	20 mins easy run
75	Warm up, 3 x 1 mile, timed, as Day 61
76	20 mins easy run
77	Rest
78	35 mins at marathon pace
79	16–18 miles endurance run. The last big one. Go easily, walk 5 mins in each hour. Time does not matter

Days 80-86

80	Rest
81	20 mins easy
82	Warm up, 3 mile timed run, as Day 68
83	40 mins steady run, marathon pace
84	Rest
85	20 mins easy
86	10 miles run, or race 6–10 miles

For last 14 days see below.

The sub-4 hr programme

Days 3-9	
3	Rest
4	5 miles, steady pace
5	10 mins easy, 10 x (30 secs fast, 60 secs slow), 10 mins easy run
6	5 miles easy run
7	Rest
8	1 mile easy, 4–5 miles good speed, 1 mile jog
9	8 miles slow run

Days 10-16	
10	Rest
11	6 miles steady pace
12	Warm-up, 10 x 30 secs uphill, jogging back, 1 mile easy
13	5–6 miles easy run
14	Rest
15	6 miles steady pace
16	10 miles endurance run

Days 17-23	
17	Rest
18	6 miles steady
19	Warm up, then 5 x (60 secs fast, 2 mins slow, 30 secs fast, 60 secs slow), then then 1–2 miles easy jog
20	6 miles easy pace
21	Rest
22	4 miles easy run
23	Warm-up, 10k race, warm down

Days 24-30	
24	5 miles easy
25	Warm-up,then 3 x 1000m fast (or 4 mins fast, 3 mins rest), warm down
26	5 miles very easy
27	Run to hill, 9 x 40 secs fast uphill, run back
28	Rest
29	Warm up, timed run as Day 1, warm down
30	12 miles slowly or 10k race

Days 31-37

31	Rest
32	6 miles Fartlek, putting in fast bursts of 150–400m
33	Warm up, 10 x 30 secs uphill, jogging back, 2 miles easy
34	5–6 miles, easy pace
35	Rest
36	6–8 miles, good pace, or 30 mins easy if racing next day
37	10 mile race or 12–15 miles steady run

Days 38-44

38	Rest
39	6 miles steady run
40	6 miles, inc. 10 x 60 secs fast, 2 mins slow
41	6 miles easy run
42	Rest
43	One hour off-road running, with changes of pace
44	11–12 miles long slow run

Days 45-51

45	Rest
46	6 miles Fartlek, with fast bursts of 200m approx
47	Warmup, 3 x 1 mile, 4 mins jog recovery, 2–3 miles easy running
48	6 miles steady pace
49	Rest
50	25 mins easy running, with a few strides
51	Half marathon race or 13 miles endurance run

Days 52-58

52	Rest
53	2 miles easy, 3 miles brisk pace, 1 mile jog
54	Warm up, 10 x 40 secs uphill, jogging back, 2 miles easy
55	6 miles easy run
56	Rest
57	7–8 miles cross-country, as you please
58	11–12 miles endurance run

Days 59-65

59	Rest
60	6 miles Fartlek, with bursts of 150–250m
61	7 miles, inc 8 x 60 secs fast and 8 x 30 secs fast
62	5 miles easy run
63	Rest
64	6 miles on grass, with some strides
65	15–16 miles endurance run – take it gently

Days 66-72

66	Rest
67	6 miles easy run
68	Warm up, 4 x 1 mile, timed, as Day 47
69	6 miles steady pace
70	Rest
71	Warm up, 4 miles at Marathon pace
72	11–13 miles steady run

Days 73-79

73	Rest
74	6 miles steady
75	6 miles Fartlek, with bursts of 200m
76	7–8 miles at marathon pace
77	4 miles easy
78	Rest
79	18 miles endurance run, taking drinks

Days 80-86

81	Rest
82	4 miles easy, off road
83	Warm up, 6 x (2 mins fast, 2 mins slow)
84	Rest
85	6 miles steady, faster if not racing next day
86	10–13 miles race or steady run

For last 14 days see below.

The sub-3 hr 30 programme

Days 3-9

3	5 miles easy
4	6 miles, starting slow, finishing strongly
5	1mile jog, 10 x (1min fast, 2mins slow), 1 mile jog
6	6 miles steady pace
7	Rest
8	5–7 miles off-road, as you feel
9	8 miles endurance run, slow pace

Days 10-16

10	5 miles easy, off-road if possible
11	1 mile easy, 3 miles brisk, 1 mile jog
12	6 miles steady pace
13	1 mile jog, 4 x (3 mins fast, 2 mins slow)
14	Rest
15	6 miles easy, off-road
16	10 miles endurance run

Days 17-23

17	5 miles easy
18	6 miles steady, with bursts of 200m
19	Run to hill, 8 x 40 secs uphill fast, jog back
20	5 miles easy
21	Rest
22	6–8 miles, off-road
23	12 miles slow endurance run, or 10k race plus warm-up and warm-down

Days 24-30

24	5 miles easy
25	Warm up, 3 x 1000m (or 4 mins), 3 mins recovery, warm down
26	5 miles very easy
27	Hill training as last week, increase to 10 x 40 secs
28	Rest
29	Warm up, timed run as Day 1, warm down
30	10k race or 12 miles slow endurance run

Days 31-37

31	5 miles easy
32	6 miles Fartlek, with bursts of 200–300m
33	Warm up, 3 x 1 mile at half marathon pace
34	6 miles, starting slow, finishing strongly
35	Rest
36	30 mins easy
37	Half marathon race or 15 miles slow endurance run

Days 38-44

38	5 miles easy, off road
39	6 miles steady, with some fast strides
40	Run to hill, 10 x 40 secs uphill fast, run back
41	7 miles steady, with a strong last mile
42	3 mile jog
43	5 miles Fartlek, grass or park
44	13 miles, easy pace

Days 45-51

45	5 miles easy
46	3 x 10 mins at half marathon pace, 4 min rests
47	4 miles easy
48	6 miles steady, with a few surges
49	Rest
50	Warm up, 3-4 miles brisk pace, warm down
51	15–16 miles endurance run. Start slowly, practice taking drinks

Days 52-58

52	4 miles easy, off road
53	5 miles easy
54	Warm up, 4 x 1 mile timed, as Day 33
55	6 miles steady run
56	Rest or 3 miles easy
57	5 miles easy on grass with 6 x 100m stride at the end
58	Half marathon race or 14–15 miles steady

Days 59-65	
59	5 miles easy, off road
60	6 miles easy Fartlek, bursts when you feel like it
61	Hill session, as Day 40
62	6 miles steady
63	Rest
64	Warm up, brisk timed run over 3–4 miles course
65	16–17 miles endurance run

Days 66-72	
66	5 miles easy, off road
67	5 miles easy, with a few strides
68	8 miles steady, about marathon pace
69	6 miles Fartlek, doing 30 secs fast, 60 secs slow
70	Rest or 3 mile jog
71	6 miles steady, including 3 miles fast if not racing
72	Race 10–13 miles, or 12–13 miles steady run

Days 73-79	
73	5 miles easy, off road
74	6 miles steady, with bursts if feeling fresh
75	7 miles Fartlek, with 10 x 1 min fast, 2 mins slow
76	6–8 miles steady
77	3 miles jogging and striding
78	Rest
79	18–20 miles endurance run, taking drinks

Days 80-86	
80	4 miles jog, off road
81	8 miles steady
82	Warm up, 6 x 800m fast (or 3 mins fast), with 2 min rests
83	6 miles easy
84	Rest
85	7 miles, including 5 miles timed, at marathon pace
86	Race 6–10 miles, or steady run, 10–12 miles

For last 14 days see below.

Try not to end up like this!

Sub-3 hr programme

This programme should cater for both the good club runner who wants to get under three hours and the more ambitious runner whose aim is to get down to under 2 hr 45. The basic princples are the same for all, but the more ambitious could put in a morning run of 30 minutes on Monday, Tuesday and Wednesday, as well as running their quality sessions that much harder. If it may seem a bit hard for the average over-40, remember that the world best for men over 40 is now 2 hr 10 minutes!

Days 3-9

3	6 miles easy, off-road if possible
4	Warm up, 4 x 1 miles at 10k pace, (3 mins recovery)
5	6 miles steady pace
6	Warm up, then 2 x (8 x 200m), with 40 secs recovery between strides and 5 minutes jog between sets
7	5 miles easy
8	5–6 miles brisk pace, cross-country or grass
9	13–15 miles endurance run

Days 10-16

10	6 miles easy, off road
11	Run to hill, 8 x 60 secs uphill fast, jog down recovery
12	6 miles steady pace
13	Interval training, track or grass. Warm up, then 6 x 800m (2mins recovery) and 6 x 400m (60 secs recovery) at 5k speed
14	5 miles easy
15	6 miles easy on grass
16	Warm up, 10k race, 3 miles warm down

Days 17-23

17	6 miles easy
18	Warm up, 1 x 2 miles, 3 x 1 mile, as Day 4
19	6 miles steady
20	7–8 miles Fartlek
21	3 mile jog
22	5 miles steady
23	16–18 miles endurance run

Days 24-30

24	6 miles easy, off road, inc. 6 x 100m fast stride at the end
25	Warm up, 8 x 1000m (or 3 mins), 2 min recoveries
26	6 miles steady
27	Hill running, as Day 11, but add one more
28	5 miles easy
29	3 miles easy Fartlek
30	Half-marathon race or 15 miles steady

Days 31-37

31	6 miles easy, off road
32	7–8 miles Fartlek, as you feel
33	Warm up, 3 x 2 miles (5 mins recovery)
34	6 miles steady, plus 8 x 100m fast stride
35	4 miles easy
36	4 miles Fartlek, with several short bursts
37	18–20 miles endurance run. Go easily, take drinks

Days 38-44

38	6 miles, starting slowly
39	Warm up, interval training – 2 sets of 8 x 400m at 5k pace, with 60 secs between runs, 3 mins between sets
40	4 miles easy
41	Run to hills, 6 x 2 mins uphill,jog back recovery
42	5 miles easy
43	5 miles easy, off road, with some strides
44	10 miles race, or good pace run, 10–12 miles

Days 45-51

45	6 miles easy, off road
46	Warm up, 1 x 2 miles, 3 x 1 mile, (5 mins recovery)
47	6 miles easy
48	8–9 miles at threshold pace
49	4 mile jog
50	6 miles on grass, inc. 8 x 100m stride
51	Two hour endurance run, taking drinks

Days 52-58

52	30 mins easy, off road
53	6 miles steady, as you feel
54	Interval training, 10 x 500m at 10k pace (90 secs recovery)
55	6 miles steady, plus 6 x 150m stride
56	4 miles easy
57	4 miles easy, inc 1 mile at race pace
58	Half marathon race or 90 mins steady run

Days 59-65

59	6 miles easy, off road
60	Warm up, 4 x 1 mile (4 mins recovery)
61	6 miles steady run
62	8 miles Fartlek, with bursts of 300–400m
63	3 mile jog
64	Rest
65	18–20 rniles endurance run, practice your pre-race preparation

Days 66-72

66	5 miles easy, off road
67	6 miles, starting slowly
68	8 miles good pace, with surges
69	8 mile run,with 10–12 x 90 secs fast, 60 secs slow
70	5 miles easy
71	6 miles Fartlek, easy run if racing
72	10k race or 11–13 miles at about marathon pace

Days 73-79

73	5 miles easy
74	6 miles easy Fartlek
75	3 miles at marathon pace, 1 mile jog, 3 miles at 10 secs/mile faster than marathon pace
76	7 miles steady, with 8 x 150m strides
77	30 mins jog
78	Rest
79	21–22 miles endurance run, taking drinks

Days 80-86

80	5 miles easy run
81	6–7 miles, starting slowly
82	Warm up, 8 x 1000m, 2 mins recovery, warm down
83	8 miles at marathon pace
84	30 mins easy jog
85	30 mins jog, with 6 x 100m strides
86	Race, 6–10 miles, or 10–12 miles steady run

The last two weeks

This is the best part of the training, because you are now in the 'tapering' phase. The harder you have trained beforehand, the more you should taper off in the last two weeks. Our rule of thumb for elite runners is to do 75% of normal mileage with three weeks to go, 50% in the penultimate week and no more than 25% in the final week. This means that the elite runner when tapering does more than the get-you-round runner does in a full week! Whatever your level, however, the principle is the same, that you are giving the body a chance to build itself up after the stresses of the previous weeks while doing just enough to stimulate the muscle enzymes and stay sharp.

In all the schedules we include a bit of fast striding in the last few days. If you have missed training and are trying to make up for it, you should still ease down over the last nine days. Putting in one more long run a week before is not recommended, because your body will not be fully recovered in time for the race. There are, however, several useful things which you can do in this period. One is to try out all your racing gear in training and another is to practice your race pace. Although your first mile time will be meaningless, because of the crowds, it is important to get the pace right in the first few miles. Practice your pace over an accurately measured road mile, or four laps of the track, wearing your racing shoes, after a suitable warm-up.

Get-You-Round Programme

Days 87-100	
87	Rest
88	20 mins easy run
89	35 mins at marathon pace
90	Warm up, 2 x 1 mile, timed
91	Rest
92	20 mins easy
93	50 mins at marathon pace
94	Rest
95	20 mins easy
96	Rest
97	10 mins warm up, then 6 x 30 secs stride, 60 secs jog
98	Rest
99	20 mins jog in racing kit
100	RACE DAY

The Sub–4 hr programme

Days 87-100	
87	Rest
88	6 miles easy
89	Warm up, 8 x 1 min fast, 2 mins slow
90	5 miles steady pace
91	Rest
92	Warm up, 3 miles at marathon pace, timed
93	10 miles steady. Practice your pre-race preparation
94	Rest
95	Warm up, 10 x 30 secs fast, 60 secs slow

96	30 mins easy, in racing shoes
97	Rest
98	Rest
99	20 mins easy, in racing kit
100	RACE DAY

The Sub-3 hr 30 programme

Days 87-100	
87	5 miles easy, off road
88	6 miles steady pace
89	Warm up, 10 x 1 min fast, 90 secs slow
90	5 miles easy
91	Rest
92	Marathon warm-up, 3 miles at marathon pace, warm down
93	10 miles, easy pace, practice marathon preparation
94	5 miles easy
95	Rest
96	30 mins easy, inc. 6 x 30 secs fast
97	Rest
98	Rest
99	20 mins easy, in racing kit
100	RACE DAY

The Sub–3 hr programme

Days 87-100	
87	6 miles easy, off road
88	6 miles Fartlek, with 8 x 1 min fast, 2 mins slow
89	1 mile easy, 4–5 miles brisk pace,1 mile jog
90	6 miles easy
91	Rest
92	Marathon warm-up, 10k at marathon pace, warm down
93	10–12 miles easy pace
94	5 miles easy
95	Rest
96	30 mins easy, inc. 1 mile at race pace, in racing shoes
97	20 mins easy, with several fast strides
98	Rest
99	20 mins easy, in racing kit
100	RACE DAY

Marathon checklist

This was our list for the Boston Centenary Marathon in 1996, which we both ran:

- Racing shoes and socks
- Trainers and socks
- Racing vest,with number attached
- Shorts
- Talcum powder and vaseline
- Tracksuit
- Waterproof jacket
- T-shirt (discardable), gloves and hat
- Dustbin liner (in case of rain before the start)
- Bottle of drink (discardable) for the start
- Chocolate bar and sweets (for afterwards)
- Plasters,scissors and antiseptic cream
- Pre-race routine

The most important bit of rehearsal is the eating routine, because most of us will be getting up earlier than usual. Aim to finish your pre-race meal three hours before the start – this allows plenty of time for digestion as well as for travelling. The meal itself should be low in fibre and easily digested – our favourite is cornflakes, boiled egg, toast and honey and a cup of tea (see Chapter 12). Having laid out the clothes the night before, get changed after breakfast, putting on plenty of layers which can be discarded later. Wear heavy trainers until you get to the start, and only change into the racing shoes before packing up your gear to go into the truck.

If the race day turns out to be hot, it is advisable to keep topping up with water from after breakfast until 30 minutes before the start, when you should get into the loo queue.It is also a good idea to have a drink two minutes before the start, if it is really hot.

Mental rehearsal

A considerable state of tension, not to say panic, ensues as we approach the race. This is normal. We would not be able to rise to a peak if we did not get nervous before a race. The best way to handle it is to plan thoroughly beforehand. Allow plenty of time to get to the start, remembering that roads will be choked and ticket offices may have queues outside. Make a note of where the loos are situated at the start and get in line before the situation gets desperate. Take special care with the rendezvous arrangements afterwards – the crowds can be appalling, and if a runner is very tired he cannot move fast. Mobile phones don't always work – writing the runners name on a piece of card and holding it up in the air is often a better way of finding someone.

Having made your plans, you go to your race with a sense of purpose. This is going to be your day, the one for which you have prepared so long, and nothing is going to spoil it. You are not going to be upset by the crowds, but you will enjoy the fellowship and make new friends. You are not going to be panicked by losing time at the start, but you will stick to your race plan, and, above all, you are not going to quit unless you are in serious pain.

Estimating your time

During the past few months you will have been getting fitter and you will have run some races. Use these to predict your marathon time, by calculating the following:

5 mile time x 6 =	
6 mile time x 5 =	(a 10k is 6.25 miles)
10 mile time x 3 =	
half marathon time x 2 + 7 1/2%	

The average of all these estimates will give you a target time. You will probably also have a 'dream time' which is better than this and a 'rock bottom' time which you need to beat to retain your self-respect.

Tactics

Remember that the marathon is a fuel economy run and try to waste as little energy as possible before and during the race. Do not waste effort trying to push past people, wait until gaps appear and slip through. Your first mile should be your slowest mile. After that try to run at level pace; if you aim to run the first ten miles as close as possible to your target time, you will still be in reach of your dream time, provided that you have done the endurance training. Once you get to halfway you are just going to keep running and try not to slow down. In our experience it is better as well as safer to aim for 'negative splits' – running the second half faster than the first. Whatever your level, go out to enjoy the experience.

The trick

If you are aiming at four hours or slower, it is well worth mixing a little walking with your running, to conserve energy, right from the start. When Bruce was pace-making in London, aiming at 3hrs 30, he overtook hundreds of people, from about the 18-mile mark onwards, who had started too fast and run out of energy. It often takes people over two hours to get from the 20 miles marker to the finish. If they had put some walking in earlier, they would be able to go on jogging and walking all the way. Walking burns up fat, of which we have plenty, and does not deplete our stores of carbohydrate, which are limited.

The sub-4 hr runner is averaging 9 minutes per mile (5:40 per km). If he runs slightly faster he can afford to walk for 2 minutes every five miles. The same applies to the 4 hr 30 and 5 hr people, whose average pace is slower than 10 mins per mile (6:20 per km). A good principle is to jog for fifty-five minutes, then walk for five.

Eating and drinking

We recommend drinking at every 5k drinks station, but in cool weather a gulp is all you will need at 5k and 10k. After that, take time to drink 50-100mls of fluid, a dilute cabohydrate drink if possible. If you can take in 500 ml of a 10% drink, that is 50g of carbohydrate, almost 200 calories, which may make all the difference between hitting the wall and keeping your pace going to the finish.

Some people take solids such as bananas during the run. If you are going fast, stick to liquids, but if you are not in a hurry you can eat your way round and never run out of energy. Italian feeding stations often have pasta and some French marathons have wine at every one!

After the race is over

This is the time when you most need to take care of yourself, or, better still, have someone else take care of you. The priorities are:

1. Take the weight off your legs.
2. Keep warm.
3. Replace fluid.
4. Replace fuel.

All these things can be done in the first five minutes after crossing the line. If you are well organised you will also have transport to take you from the finish to somewhere where you can shower and rest as soon as possible. Do not put yourself into a situation where you have to drive yourself, because stiffness, tiredness and cramp could make you a very dangerous driver indeed.

We suggest that you take no exercise apart from walking until a week after the race. Trying to run on stiff muscles is painful and there is no evidence that it does any good.

Richard Cashmore

age: **64** started running at: **44** occupation: **businessman**

"I was inspired to start running by the first London Marathon in 1981, when I was 44. Limited preparation got me round the 1982 Birmingham marathon in 3 hr 48, walking the last few miles. I was hooked. Three more marathons in 1982 saw me improve to 3 hr 09, walking less each time, and then in March '83 I broke through to 2 hr 51 – I was no longer a jogger!"

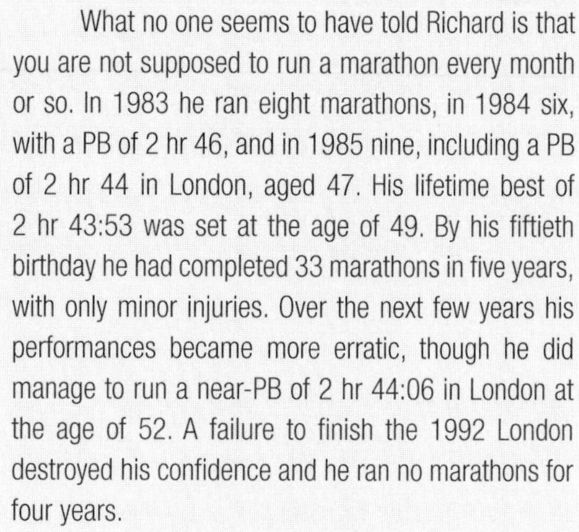

What no one seems to have told Richard is that you are not supposed to run a marathon every month or so. In 1983 he ran eight marathons, in 1984 six, with a PB of 2 hr 46, and in 1985 nine, including a PB of 2 hr 44 in London, aged 47. His lifetime best of 2 hr 43:53 was set at the age of 49. By his fiftieth birthday he had completed 33 marathons in five years, with only minor injuries. Over the next few years his performances became more erratic, though he did manage to run a near-PB of 2 hr 44:06 in London at the age of 52. A failure to finish the 1992 London destroyed his confidence and he ran no marathons for four years.

"Eventually my 60th birthday approached and with it the challenge of a new age group (are we runners the only people who almost welcome the passing of the years?) Previously self-coached from books and magazines, I sought the advice of Sally Ellis, our local Olympic marathon runner.

"Sally devised a programme which included track sessions, tempo runs, heart-rate monitoring, recovery, discipline and encouragement. My enthusiasm returned and under this regime I managed consecutive Londons in 2 hr 57, 3 hr 03, 2 hr 58 and 3 hr 05 – my fiftieth marathon at the age of 62.

"What turned a sedentary, non-competitive businessman into an addicted marathon runner? Mainly the discovery that I possessed some natural ability and stamina, plus the fact that the mental strength which comes with middle age is an essential marathon requirement.

"In my early days, my motivation came from continuous improvement and even the eventual decline was softened by age-group competition. To this can be added the camaraderie and goodwill that one finds in this totally classless activity. Neither wealth, influence nor privilege have any effect on performance. We differ only in the amount of natural ability we possess and the extent to which we can develop it."

What we would all like to know is how you can run eight goodish marathons in a year without getting chronically injured. Richard puts this down to a light build and a balanced gait. He doesn't do cross-country because he doesn't like slippery or uneven surfaces, but on the road he can relax into an 'automatic' pace.

CHAPTER TWELVE

Lifestyle, health and diet

The late Dr. George Sheehan, one of the gurus of our sport, said: "It is a good thing to be an athlete at forty, but when you are seventy it's essential." This was a typical Sheehan remark – funny, apparently controversial, but actually founded on good sense. Most people outside the running world would consider it ridiculous for a man of seventy to consider himself an athlete, but Sheehan's point was that the seventy-year-old athlete really knows his body and takes good care of it.

We have to tread a careful path between extremes. We should be concerned about our health, but not worry too much. We all know the hypochondriac runner, who is never happy unless he has found some interesting complaint from which he suffers – and which he forces the rest of us to suffer. Extreme self-obsession makes you a very boring person. We should be relaxed about the way we live, but not careless. It makes no sense to train for weeks for an event and then rule yourself out by straining your back the day before.

Running should add to your life, not restrict it. The person who is fully fit can cope with life better, eat and drink what he likes and generally enjoy life more than the unfit person.

Running through life

Remember the old saying – "if you don't want to lose it, use it". Exercise is good, sloth is bad – except when you have done your exercise and you can really enjoy being slothful without feeling guilty. The runner will run up the stairs rather than use the lift. Over any distance under a mile, the runner will go on foot rather than drive – the difference in time is marginal.

You arrive in a new place and unpack your bag. You've had a tiring journey and there is an hour to go before dinner. Do you lie down for half an hour and then go to the bar, do you go out and walk a mile or two, or do you get changed and run for three or four miles? The answer you give is an indicator of your physical, rather than historical, age.

Running and Working

The things which makes you a successful runner – will-power, dedication, the determination to improve – will also make you a successful person in your professional life, and thus may well lead to a conflict of interests. If you are ambitious you want to start earlier, work a bit later, put in that extra visit, and this leaves you less time for running. You will say: "I'll just run a bit more tomorrow, or the next day, or at the weekend", and then another commitment comes up and you miss the whole week, so you are left with more running to do to catch up, and less time to do it in.

The first thing we would say is: "Don't be afraid to run." If the President of the USA can find time for a daily run, so can you. If a business does not realise that a fit disciplined employee is a lot more valuable than a Mr Blobby, then you are in the wrong business. A good firm should provide somewhere to change and shower, so that you can fit in a run before work or in the lunch hour.

> **"Sometimes I would run home from my office at 10 pm after a long day, and it would take me 3 miles to clear my head. How can you enjoy your running when you are under the hammer at work and at home?"**
>
> KEVIN SHANNON

What you will have to do is to strike a compromise between the intensity of your work and the intensity of your training. When things are really hectic, you may have to cut back to two short runs during the working week, but with plenty of running at the weekend – and an eye on your diet – you can stay very fit.

Let your running be your therapy. There will be times when you want to go out and push yourself to work off frustration and times when you just want to run peacefully and think about nothing at all, so ignore the schedule – retaining your sanity is more important.

What is important is continuity. Keep it going. Even running twice a week will keep you fit and is much better than letting it go completely. When you retire you will have plenty of time for running, but it will be much harder to get back if you haven't run for the previous decade.

Running keeps you healthy

Diet

It is not true that 'you are what you eat'. Primarily, you are what you are – depending on your genes – and secondarily, you modify your body by your level of activity.

If a pair of identical twins were eating identical diets and one was, say, a professional cyclist, riding for five or six hours a day, while the other spent most of the day in front of a computer or a TV screen, the cyclist would be lean and fit with big leg muscles, while the sedentary one would be soft and pudgy, with more sub-cutaneous fat, weak muscles and an under-developed cardio-vascular system. With the same genes and the same food intake, one would be eating just enough and the other would be over-eating. The most important thing about food is that it provides the fuel for the energy you consume. If you take in more than you burn up, you get fatter. If you burn up more than you take in, you get thinner.

The next most important thing about food is that it provides the building blocks for repair and development, as well as for the enzymes and the hormones which control our development and maintain a constant internal environment. Hence, a lack of something in your diet may upset your equilibrium or prevent you recovering quickly after a hard effort. The lack of certain nutrients may weaken your immune system, making you more likely to pick up infections when under stress.

The third important thing about food is that it must taste good. Eating is one of life's greatest pleasures and working up an appetite by running makes it even more pleasurable. Moreover, If you don't enjoy your meals then you probably won't eat a balanced diet. This is not a cookery book, so you won't find any recipes, but the best cuisines are those where the food is freshly produced and freshly cooked. The shorter the time from garden to table, the better it tastes and the more good it does, because there are fewer preservatives and the vitamins have not been destroyed by over-cooking.

Weight loss and exercise

Dieting without exercise is worse than useless. You probably realise that, or you wouldn't have bought this book. We can assume that the sedentary person eats slightly more per day than he really needs. The excess fuel is converted and stored as fat under the skin. If we drastically cut down our food intake through dieting we will burn up some of that fat to provide us with our daily energy needs, and so lose weight. However, the naturally sedentary person, feeling weak through lack of food, will take even less exercise than usual, so his muscles will get even weaker and smaller. When the person relapses to eating his normal diet, without taking extra exercise, the extra weight is regained as fat, not as muscle.

> **"I follow no specific diet, but I tend to eat a lot of carbohydrate and a lot of fruit and salads. I do not eat red meat, but I eat chicken and fish. I drink very little alcohol - about one glass of wine a week! Before morning races I always have Weetabix with honey, as well as toast. I try to eat pasta for lunch and dinner the day before a long race."**
>
> **JENNY GRAY,** BRITISH VETS CHAMPION AND WORLD BRONZE MEDALLIST

The best solution is to increase the exercise level a little and decrease the food intake a little. There is a very simple weight-loss exercise. Simply press the lips firmly together and move the chin first to the right, then to the left. Repeat this exercise rapidly, twice in each direction, whenever someone offers you a second helping. The other easy ways of cutting down the calorie intake are:

1. Cut down on sugar in tea and coffee (10g of sugar is 39 calories).
2. Cut down on butter and marge on your food (10g of butter is 73 calories).
3. Cut out crisps before meals, chocolate and biscuits after meals.
4. Stick to three meals a day with no sugary snacks in-between.

Setting targets

Suppose you have put on five pounds over the Christmas holidays. Give yourself five weeks to get this down. If a pound of fat represents twenty miles of running, you need to increase your running a little and cut down the calorie intake a little.

Women have more trouble controlling their weight than men, because their energy consumption is often much lower, for a variety of reasons, but the same principles apply – burn more fuel and take in a little less.

What athletes eat

One big advantage of being a runner is that you can eat a lot without putting on weight.For some of us it is the main reason for running!

The more you run, the more you can eat. The needs of the average sedentary man can be met by 2500 calories a day. The calorie need for an average woman would be around 2100 per day, mainly because the woman weighs less. A runner putting in 10 miles a day can consume at least an extra 1000 calories a day – We say 'at least', because running speeds up your metabolism, so that after you have been running you continue to burn up fuel at a faster rate.

We do not believe that diet has very much to do with athletic performance. The proof of this is that you can take a World Championships field and find amongst it people of widely different cultures, with enormous differences in their dietary habits, yet the differences in their performances are measured in fractions of a percentage point. There is nothing you can eat which can make you run faster, but we will accept that a diet which is consistently deficient in certain vitamins and minerals will limit your performance. One of the spin-offs of eating a large amount of food is that one is very unlikely to suffer from a deficiency of any of the trace elements. Let's look at the way we tackle certain practical problems from the point of view of the hard-training runner who is averaging 10 miles a day.

The regular daily diet

As long as you emphasise variety, you should cover all the the necessary vitamins and minerals, and the problem may be just one of preparing and eating enough in a day to get the necessary calories. Our rules are:

i) Each meal should include either fresh fruit or salad, or both.
ii) Each meal should include a major source of carbohydrates, which can be added to as necessary.
iii) Water should be taken immediately after each training session and some food as soon as possible afterwards.

The hard-training athlete may need as much as 4000 calories a day and since 60–70% of those calories should come from carbohydrates he should be eating over 500 grams of carbohydrates a day. A large plateful of rice or pasta represents about 4oz (112g) of the food in its dry form, which is mostly carbohydrate. The high-mileage athlete needs to eat four or five times this amount per day, depending on how big he or she is and how much training is being done. When we are in a training camp, the daily menu looks like this:

Breakfast

fruit juice or fresh fruit, porridge or muesli, toast and marmalade, a banana, tea or coffee

Lunch

soup, with a lot of bread, pasta with a simple sauce, green salad or coleslaw

Supper

fish, chicken or meat dish, with large amounts of rice, potatoes or pasta and a green vegetable; fruit salad or rice pudding, tea or coffee

In addition to this we often have a drink and a banana right after training. Most runners drink at least half a pint of water or dilute juice immediately after each training session, and when the mileage is really high they drink high-carbohydrate drinks such as High Five or Leppin, where you mix the powder in with the water.

We have made no specific mention of fibre content here, because by eating a lot of fresh fruit and vegetables we get all the fibre we need. The same goes for proteins, because in addition to the protein foods of the main course, there is an appreciable amount of protein in bread, potatoes and pasta

Travelling

A big problem for the modern sportsman is that he is taken away far too often from his stable environment, where he is probably getting an adequate diet and forced to buy food, often from fast-food outlets at stations and airports. The guidelines here are:

i) Take a packed meal with you, so that you can get what you want.
ii) Carry a water bottle with water or dilute juice in it, so that you don't get dehydrated.
iii) Carry a reserve of fruit and chocolate and/or muesli bars.
iv) Try to eat a small meal every 3–4 hours, rather than starving for hours and then stuffing yourself when you arrive.

Pre-race meals

The bottom line is being fit

This is where it's easy to make mistakes. Athletes, being very nervous, often don't feel like eating, but on the other hand some people eat too close to the competition, then find that their food does not digest as quickly as usual.

You should finish your meal between three hours and five hours before the start time of your race. If you have breakfast at eight and your race is, say one o'clock, that is fine, but if your event is at two-thirty we would recommend having a drink and a snack at eleven. Incidentally, you can go on drinking right up to the start of your race, and in hot weather we would recommend this. Use plain water, squash or an isotonic drink, but avoid taking a lot of tea or coffee because of their diuretic effect. The right things to eat at this stage are those which are easily digested, low in fibre, with a high carbohydrate content.

Recommended foods: White bread or toast, ripe bananas, honey sandwiches, chocolate bars, low-bran cereals such as cornflakes or rice crispies.

Foods to avoid: High-fibre foods such as muesli, fatty foods such as fish and chips, milk shakes, fried bacon

Post-race meals

After a big effort your body is dehydrated and your muscles are low in glycogen. The first need is to replace the fluid, and we would recommend an isotonic drink here, unless you have been running a very long way, in which case a high-carbohydrate drink is best.

If you can put back some of the fuel within the first hour after the exercise your recovery rate will be much quicker. The enzymes which were used to break down the glycogen are the same ones that bring about the re-synthesis of glycogen, and they are present in high concentrations in the muscle cells immediately after the exercise – so take in some simple carbohydrate food as soon as you can tolerate it.

Special events

If you are running a marathon or taking part in an event which goes on for several hours, your requirements are somewhat different. For a start, because you will be be exercising at a slower rate for some of the time it is alright to have some fat in the meal at the beginning of the day -provided you have time to digest it. It is also a good thing to keep on snacking every hour-and-a-half, so that your glycogen stores can be topped up, and it is essential to keep taking fluids. This is where the commercial replacement drinks come into their own and you should choose one which has a balance of water and salts, plus enough carbohydrate to meet your energy needs, but not so much that it upsets your digestion. In a marathon, you should be taking drinks every three miles, and in a long-running sport you should take drinks at least every half-hour if possible.

Carboloading

There is definite evidence that you can store up extra glycogen just before a long endurance event, if you take in extra carbohydrate at the right time. In the last few days before a marathon you will be tapering off your training, running three or four miles a day instead of ten, hence you will tend to build up your stores even without eating anything special. If you are competing in a marathon on a Sunday, we recommend that the last bit of effort – a brisk six or seven miles – should come on Tuesday afternoon, and after that the runner eats only smallish amounts of carbohydrate for the next 48 hours. Excessive depletion is dangerous. From the Thursday evening, for 48 hours, he should take large amounts of carbohydrate – 10 grams of carbohydrate per kilo of body weight per day and large amounts of water. This will cause him to put on weight. On the Saturday he should have only a normal evening meal, so as not to upset his digestive system, and the following morning he should have a normal breakfast. The extra glycogen stored can make all the difference to the runner's energy reserves. If you add on the amount you can take in in energy drinks during the race it means that you can run fast all the way without hitting the wall.

Proteins

We do need protein, but not in excessive amounts. The recommendation for active athletes is just over 1g of protein for every 1kg of body weight, which means 70–80g of protein per day. This can come equally well from vegetarian or non-vegetarian sources. Remember that there is protein in bread, cereals and many vegetables, as well as in the traditional meat, fish, eggs and milk.

Fats

Fats are excellent sources of energy, and for that reason it is easy to eat more fat than we need. For the average person, fats should provide no more than 25–30% of total energy and for hard-training athletes the figure should be less than 20%.

Iron

For women runners in particular, anaemia can be a recurring problem, so apart from having regular blood checks, we recommend that you talk to your doctor about taking a course of iron tablets, if necessary.

Salt

We were sending marathon training advice to a runner, and all was going well, with personal bests being set at the shorter distances. When it came to the marathon, he was right on schedule until he got very bad cramp and had to drop out. It turned out that he took no salt in his diet. Sodium, Potassium and Chloride ions, known as 'electrolytes' are essential to our diet. There is usually more than enough salt (sodium chloride) in our diet, and if you are taking plenty of fruit and fruit juices you will also have plenty of potassium.

Sports drinks and supplements

Most of the time, plain water will do fine, because you get the salts and glucose in your daily diet. When exercising for a long time, we recommend an isotonic drink – which contains the same concentrations of salts as your sweat, with a small amount of carbohydrate. However, if you are burning up a lot of fuel, you will need a high-carbohydrate drink. You can make up your own, by mixing sugar, salt, water and juice, or you can buy one. The carbohydrate concentration should not be higher than 10%, because the stomach can't handle it. In hotter weather you will drink more, so the concentration can be lower – about 6–7%.

There are many other expensive supplements on the market, mostly containing proteins and various amino-acids. Others contain a cocktail of vitamins and minerals. The evidence that they improve performance is pretty flimsy and the differences would only be fractions of a percentage point. There is a case for taking multi-vitamin pills if you think you might be deficient in something. Our recommendation is that you put yourself onto a 30-day course of multi-vitamins and see if it makes any difference. There are two products which we recommend for our elite athletes – glutamine, taken after long hard races or very hard training efforts, which helps to boost the immune system and decreases your chances of picking up a virus, and glucosamine, which is good for protecting against damage to joints.

Diet: a summary

Rather than become obsessed by diet, it is best to stick to a few basic guidelines, as follows:

1. Use your weight as a guide. You should weigh no more at sixty than you weighed at thirty.
2. Eat regularly, at least three times a day. If you are training hard you may need four small meals rather than three larger ones.
3. All meals should be predominantly carbohydrate-based (bread, cereals, rice, pasta).
4. Eat fruit or take fruit juice with every meal.
5. Eat salad or fresh vegetables at least once a day.
6. Drink plenty of water.

Vegetarians

Humans evolved as omnivores. If you are a vegetarian you may find it more difficult to get all the aminoacids and vitamins which are normally present in meat, but it can be done and there are a number of top-class athletes who are vegetarians. The world's best distance runners, the Kenyans, have a diet which is low in meat and high in carbohydrates, but they do drink a lot of milk.

Sex and drugs and rock'n'roll

It used to be thought that abstaining from sex made athletets more aggressive and hence made them perform better, but few would subscribe to that theory nowadays. An athlete performs better when he has a happy and stable background, and as long as he has the time to concentrate on the event. Having sex the night before a race may even be a good thing, because you sleep better afterwards.

The most popular drugs – alcohol and tobacco – will certainly affect performance, but only when used in the wrong way. Alcohol is broken down by the body, quite quickly, at the rate of one unit per hour, and if you are burning up a lot of calories in training you will not put on excess weight from drinking either One distance runner we know drank a bottle of wine every day – but he was running 25 miles every day as well. Our advice is to drink only in the evening, after training, because if you drink at lunchtime you will notice the effects. If you have at least one alcohol-free day per week, you can be sure that there will be no build-up of alcohol in the blood.

What you drink does not matter – it is the total number of units per day which counts. If you have had a lot to drink and have a hangover, drink plenty of water, because it is the dehydration which is the main cause of the hangover. Trying to 'run it off' without taking water will only make it worse.

Cigarettes are different, because the effects are cumulative. Not only can the tars cause lung cancer, but the rate of air-flow decreases for every cigarette smoked. The smallest air passages in the lung become inflamed, and you cannot get oxygen into your blood as quickly as a non-smoker. Smoking does not affect sprinters, because they do not depend on oxygen, but it will definitely slow you down if you are running any distance longer than 400m.

Rock and roll will do you no harm at all, unless you get beaten up at a rock concert. Any kind of dancing is good exercise, and an energetic rock or jazz evening can be counted as an extra training session.

Jenny Mills

age: **52** occupation: **retired teacher**
personal bests (over-50): **10 miles** 67:27
half marathon 87:09 **marathon** 3 hr 25

"My introduction to running was at about the age of eight, running after lambs and bullocks, with myself on one side, the dog on the other and father at the back shouting: 'stop that one over there' (usually the wiliest and fastest quadruped in the flock). I have always loved the feeling of running, because I need to expend large amounts of energy. Since I live way out in the Devon countryside and I'm not a team person I can just go for a run and enjoy the scenery.

"I didn't join a club until I was nearly 45, but I love the competition. I love going to races, meeting all my mates from other clubs and seeing different places.

"You may feel that my approach is not technical enough – I just run as I feel in training and in races. I'm lucky to be able to do my running in the middle of the morning, which suits me best – I'm too tired at the end of the day to do much useful training.

"I don't race shorter distances because of a circulatory problem. In half marathons I just run as fast as I can and in marathons I ease off if I'm feeling tired and speed up if I'm feeling good. I'd like to reassure older people thinking of running that they don't have to time every session, don't have to chase PBs and don't have to train for months on end for a marathon; just treat them as an adventure and you'll have a brilliant day out.

"I can't really choose a single highlight. Out of 81 races in the past 2½ years I've been privileged to come in the top three in 47 of them, and all of them gave me a thrill. I loved the Clarendon Way (off-road), the Cornish Marathon and the 5-4-3-2-1 event (not a race) organised by Salisbury fire station.

"The Revelstoke coastal run in South Devon is wonderfully scenic and quirky. The course goes along the foreshore, up the slipway and into the pub, where you take your number off and give it back for next year. Everyone gets a medal, presented by the vicar, and that's it! Despite the absence of prizes, well over 100 runners enter, and this sums up the sheer fun of the sport for me.

"I feel that as you get older it is essential to keep on moving your goalposts, otherwiseyou are going to get frustrated. I have seen a lot of people suffer because they can't cope with getting slower. They train harder and harder to stay in the same place, and eventually they crash."

CHAPTER THIRTEEN

Injuries and ailments

> *"If I train too hard I get injured, and if I race without having done any training I get injured."*
>
> CHRIS ROWLEY

How to avoid injury

From our questionnaires, the most frequent comment was: "Injuries and niggles seem to crop up more frequently as I get older". When we realise that muscles and ligaments lose their elasticity as we get older, this is hardly surprising, but there are remedies, and a few people were able to report that they seldom get injured.

A man's greatest strength is often his greatest weakness and this is particularly noticeable amongst athletes. The compulsive streak in their character which drives them to train hour after hour, day after day, is their worst enemy when it comes to handling injuries. The obsessive runner is all too apt to go out 'just to try it out' well before the injury has cleared up, resulting in further injury. Some veteran runners seem to have learned from their mistakes and some do not. The next most frequent comment in the questionnaires was: "it takes me longer than it used to to recover from a hard session."

The best thing is not to get injured in the first place which means putting 'avoidance of injury' high on the list of priorities. When we are making out training plans we always start by listing the objectives – such things as 'improving aerobic fitness', 'maintaining endurance' and 'maintaining flexibility'. Putting 'avoidance of injury' on this list keeps it at the forefront of the mind when planning the week's training. These are the guidelines:

1. Never train hard when stiff from the previous effort.
2. Introduce new activities very gradually.
3. Allow lots of time for warming up and cooling down.
4. Check over training and competition courses beforehand.
5. Train on different surfaces during the week, using the right footwear for each one.
6. Shower and change immediately after the cool-down.
7. Aim for the maximum comfort when travelling.
8. Stay away from infectious areas when training or competing very hard.
9. Be extremely fussy about hygiene in hot weather.
10. Maintain your all-round muscular development.
11. Have at least one non-running day in the week.
12. Monitor yourself daily for signs of fatigue. If in doubt, ease off.

Never train hard when stiff

This seems obvious,but it is seen all too often at the beginning of a season or in a training camp. Some people turn up very fit and set a fast pace in training – and the others suffer for it the next day – but instead of waiting for the stiffness to ease off they try to go on training as hard as the day before. Stiffness is caused by the leakage of tissue fluid, causing tightness in the compartments which enclose the muscle fibres. If muscles cannot contract without pain, running becomes awkward, movements are not co-ordinated and injuries are more likely.

Introduce new activities gradually

Ideally, one would never introduce anything new at all, but there are bound to be changes of emphasis – the switch from indoor to outdoor training or from grass to a synthetic surface. The solution is to start switching well before it is necessary. In switching from cross-country running to the synthetic track, for example, one might include a bit of running on the track whenever the opportunity arises, even if it is only three or four laps and a few strides after a steady run. The first track session of the year would only be half a normal session, and it

> **"I think that the vast majority of injuries I suffered occurred because I did not have the time to train. Now, at 58, I can pick my time of day to train and rest when I need it. For the very first time I am actually enjoying it and really looking forward to the next race."**
>
> KEVIN SHANNON

would be done mostly in trainers. The following week one might do most of one session on the track, but only part of it in spikes, and for the next two weeks one increases the proportion done in spikes. After a month we might be running three times a week on the track, with other sessions being done mostly on grass.

Warming up and cooling down

In the British climate this is particularly necessary. Warm muscles stretch much more easily than cold muscles. Ligaments and tendons are more likely to tear when the muscles are cold and inflexible, and of course this applies even more forcibly to the older athletes, where the tissues have become less elastic than they were. The warm-up procedure helps in several other ways too, both physically, in diverting the blood flow from non-essential areas to working muscles and mentally, in focussing the mind on the job to be done. Very often, particularly in winter, one goes out with reluctance, not feeling like training hard, but after ten minutes of easy running to warm up one feels more enthusiastic.

We would recommend at least fifteen minutes and up to thirty minutes warm-up before hard training starts. In training for ball games this can often be done with a ball, carrying out various skill routines, but in all cases it should start with five to ten minutes of gentle movement, gradually increasing in pace, followed by five to ten minutes of stretching, still in warm clothing. After that one moves to fast strides and eventually to short sprints, then stays warm and loose until the start. A sprinter might well take forty-five minutes to warm up for a ten-second burst of energy. During the cool-down period,which should last for ten to fifteen minutes after a competition or a hard training session, the body temperature returns to normal and the fatigue products are flushed out of the muscles, which reduces the chances of stiffness the next day. This is also the right time to do your stretching exercises (see Appendix 1.)

Check the course beforehand

In cross-country and road running there may be unexpected traps for the unwary – potholes in the road, sudden ups or downs, all of which could cause trouble if you are not prepared for them, and of course this is closely linked to the next rule:

Wear the right shoes

Wearing shoes which are too light and flimsy or which are unevenly worn are two very common causes of injury. If you turn up expecting a soft course and find that it is frozen hard you could be in a lot of trouble. Bruce once arrived for a so-called cross-country race in Madrid to find that it was 90% road; luckily he had brought his road racing shoes, but his England colleague, who had only spikes, had to run the race in dance shoes strapped on with pink ribbon! At a

In the best shape of their lives – World Veterans Championships in Brisbane

higher level, Liz McColgan threw away her chance of winning the World cross-country title in Boston in 1992, because she had not checked out the length of spikes necessary on the snow-covered course. Perhaps the commonest cause of all injuries is training too much on hard surfaces. In the spring of 2001, when the foot and mouth epidemic closed the fields and footpaths, there were far more people suffering from Achilles tendon problems, through running entirely on the road. Running fast on roads and tartan tracks causes a lot of impact shock. It is vital that you have trainers which will protect you – and we also recommend getting off the road onto a softer surface at least one day in three.

Shower and change after training

This reduces the likelihood of stiffening up and your chances of catching a cold.

Aim for comfort when travelling

The first thing is to give yourself adequate time to get to your race venue (which means knowing exactly where it is). Sitting in a cramped position for hours before a race is not a good thing. Aim to get up and walk around once an hour. If possible, give yourself space to stretch out. For journeys lasting several hours, take water with you and a bit of fruit and chocolate to keep up your energy levels. If you are running a marathon, make sure that you have got someone to drive you home afterwards.

Stay away from infections

This is particularly important immediately after a race or a very hard training session, when you are feeling tired and run-down

Be fussy about hygiene

Again, this matters most when you are training really hard. Things like washing hands regularly, cleaning pans, plates and cutlery thoroughly and not eating stale food are all a part of taking good care of yourself.

Maintain all-round muscular development

Injuries to joints often happen because the muscles around the joint are not strong enough to keep the joint firm when stress is placed on it. The older we get, the more our muscle strength declines (about 0.5% per year) and the more nece-saary it becomes to do regular strengthening exercises (see Appendix 2.)

Have at least one non-running day in the week

Running injuries are often repetitive strain injuries, so if you avoid running one day it gives your body almost 48 hours of recovery. If you have to take exer-cise, make it something quite different – cycling, yoga, swimming, weight training.

Monitor yourself

Another important adage is: "if in doubt, ease off". If you are feeling tired in training day after day for a whole week, if you feel dizzy or feverish, or if your resting pulse rate is ten beats or more above normal, don't go out running that day. Listen to your body and do not allow your dedication to regular running to over-ride commonsense.

How to stay fit when injured

An injured sportsman is like a sick gorilla – no use and a lot of trouble. The coach has to deal with the mind as well as the body in maintaining the athlete's equilib-rium. We heard a story about one our leading middle-distance runners who went out to a training camp and injured himself on the first day. "Right," he said, "I'm on my holidays now", and off he went to the pool hall for the next week. This approach scores high marks for relaxation but very few for intelligence. The first thing to do, obviously, is to get treatment, but the very next thing is to redesign the programme and start on rehabilitation. A few days away from the regular training routine can have a beneficial effect, particularly if the athlete has been training very hard. The injury may force him to take the rest which the body needs and he will be much better for it. However, total inactivity is a bad thing, particularly since most sportsmen are accustomed to an organised programme and may lose their sense of direction if deprived of it.

> **"In my view, most runners don't change their training once they become vets. Those who trained like crazy and without science continue to do so, while the more thoughtful runners continue to use their brains rather than brawn."**
>
> TERRY McCARTHY

The first step is to decide which movements the injury will and will not allow. If we take for an example a lower leg injury to a runner – shin splints or a stress fracture – then running itself is ruled out as an exercise and so are sports which involve running on hard surfaces. However, it should be possible to construct a programme which will train most of the attributes of a runner, so that he can go straight back to running when the injury has cleared up. It may even be possible to improve his capabilities in some respects – those things which he has not had time for. The things which make him a good runner are:

A. An efficient cardiovascular system.
B. A good power to weight ratio.
C. Strong leg muscles.
D. Good local muscular endurance.
E. Good general endurance.
F. Above average flexibility.
G. Strong motivation to succeed.

There are several good ways of maintaining cardiovascular fitness, so you should choose the ones which put no strain on the injury. Gym work is probably the safest thing, using static bicycles, rowing machines or Nordic ski machines. Mountain biking is excellent if the injury allows it. If you can only do non-weight-bearing exercises then you have to turn to swimming. The most effective way of staying fit in the pool is by wearing a 'wet-vest' and doing interval training – alternating minutes of running on the spot with minutes of slow paddling. Whatever method you use, the heart rate monitor is a great help in these situations, because you can push yourself up into the right training zone. If you don't use a monitor, measure your resting pulse rate every day to reassure yourself that you are not losing fitness.

For attribute B you need to weigh yourself regularly, to watch the food intake and to burn off enough calories in the various types of exercise to keep your weight down to its normal level.

For attribute C – muscular strength – weight training using fixed resistance, as in the Multigym, Schnell or Nautilus systems, is the best thing, but the other activities will all help. The attraction of weight training is that it is measurable and the athlete can work to a schedule and see that he is actually improving both his strength and his endurance in the exercises he is allowed to do.

Attribute D may present problems, as you will be unable to use exactly the same action in training as you would in running. Cycling on a cycle ergometer is probably the best thing here, as it works the leg muscles hard. Using these machines you can increase the resistance and follow a definite programme, so that you can see that you are making progress.

General Endurance, attribute E, allows plenty of variety, but we would choose walking as the best activity, wearing boots and walking on soft ground to prevent any shock to the injury. The advantage of a prolonged low-intensity exercise is that it is therapeutic, it allows the athlete time to think, it calms him down and gives him the assurance that he is doing something positive.

F is for Flexibility, something in which many athletes are lacking. The important thing here is continuity. A series of exercises, depending on the injury, should be planned to last fifteen to twenty minutes a day, generally after some other type of exercise to get the muscles warm. It should be possible for the athlete to be more flexible at the end of the rehab course than he was before the injury. A typical weekly programme might take the following form:

Monday-Friday	
mornings:	15 mins on static bike or rowing machine, followed by 10–15 mins flexibility exercises
Monday	
lunchtime:	15 mins weight training in gym evening: walk or cycle to pool, 20 mins swim
Tuesday	
evening:	60 mins cycling,with several hard bursts up hills
Wednesday	
	as Monday, but include 6–8 x (running in wet vest, 1 min fast, one min slow)
Thursday	
	60 mins fast walk, in boots, plus light jogging
Friday	
	Rest

Saturday

2–3 hours walking, with 5 mins flexibility exercises each hour

Sunday

60 mins hard cycling, 20 mins steady swim, 30 mins walk/jog

The last attribute, of course, is the very one which makes it possible for him to work on such a programme, even though he may not be able to train at his usual sport. A few years ago we got to know Dieter Baumann, the Olympic 5000metres champion in Barcelona. He suffered an ankle injury at the beginning of the 1993 season and was unable to do any serious training. He kept up a programme of cycling, swimming and gym work right through the summer and kept his fitness so that he was able to get back to off-road and off-track running in the 1993/94 winter. Whereas a lesser athlete might have been discouraged by being unable to race, the strength of character which enabled him to win the Olympic title in 1992 put him back on the track in 1994, fit enough to win the Europa Cup 5000m in his first major race. As with other forms of training, the way to make a long rehabilitation period tolerable is to periodise it, spending, say, six weeks on weight and ergometer training, moving on as mobility improves, to pool and bicycle training, and setting specific targets for these, over a period of three or four weeks. Specific flexibility exercises, as recommended by the doctor and the physio, will be part of the programme almost every day. Walking should be started as soon as it is safe, and this can move onto slow jogging on soft surfaces, then running slowly up a gentle slope.

> **"Savour it rather than suffer it, that's my attitude. What a privilege it is to be up and running."**
>
> RALPH HENLEY

However thorough the rehab. training has been, it will take time to get back to your best performance level, because you cannot duplicate the hardest running sessions. Once you are back to normal training, allow at least a week of training for every week that you have been rehabilitating, before you start to compete.

Whatever the injury, athlete and coach should never give up. The training of the will which comes from overcoming adversity will make the athlete much stronger in the competitive situation.

The older you get, the more likely you are to get injured and so the more careful you have to be in coming back into competition. There may well come a time when it is best not to compete, in the sense of pushing yourself to the limit, but to run at the pace which suits you, regardless of what others in the race are doing. The Bob Pape story (see below) is a good example. When he was in his forties and fifties he was running thirty races or more per year. The year he was sixty he ran 13 races, at seventy only two – but at seventy-seven he is still running.

Bob Pape

age: **77** occupation: **retired Naval officer**

Bruce: "When I was a young man doing National Service in Hong Kong, I won the colony 5000m title. I thought I was quite good until Bob Pape, the Navy runner, came on the scene. In the heat of Hong Kong he ran a world best time for thirty miles (2 hr 54 mins), and I realised what hard training could do."

Bob had his first serious race in 1939, soon after joining the Royal Navy as a boy seaman, and he had his last race sixty years later. In between those times he enjoyed considerable success, chiefly at the longer distances. A turning point in his career came in 1952, when he raced against Jim Peters, then the world record-holder for the marathon. Peters advised him to double his training, and to keep a record of all training and racing. From then on up to the age of forty, he pushed his training up to five thousand miles a year, which brought him several marathon titles and his world best for 30 miles. At the age of 35 he finished 6th in the Boston Marathon in 2 hr 28. At 50 he was still running 60 miles a week, and won the British vets 10000m title. In all this time he was seldom injured, and never out for more than 10 days – something which can probably be put down to his excellent all-round muscle development. Two events which might have been catastrophic for a lesser man – a burst appendix and peritonitis when he was 45 and a brain tumour when he was sixty – were merely temporary interruptions in his running; his fitness enabled him to recover quickly and in both cases he was back running again six weeks later.

"I always enjoyed running and would train twice or even three times a day when it was possible. I said that I'd retire when I ceased to enjoy it or when I became too stiff to run, but it hasn't happened, and at 77 I'm still jogging every day.

"My policy has been to train hard only when I feel like it, and to run relaxed if I'm not feeling so good."

The benefits of this attitude are shown by the fact that he has had fewer injuries as the years have gone by, rather than more.

CHAPTER FOURTEEN
The final chapter

> *"The grave's a fine and private place,*
> *but none, I think, do there embrace"*
>
> JOHN DONNE

A runner dreamed that he died and went into Purgatory, where he met other disembodied souls. He asked them: "What is the after-life like?"

One said: "It's hell, you have to run every day." The other said: "It's heaven, you can run as much as you want."

We are going to avoid theological discussion here, but as far as the body is concerned, the next stage beyond being a very old athlete is a dead athlete. Although the prospect of eternal rest may be attractive, the questions we should be asking ourselves are: "Should we stop running?" and "What is the best recipe for a long and healthy life?"

What must be acknowledged is that with increasing lifespan, those of us who live to seventy can expect to be around for at least another decade, or maybe two. Does this put a different complexion on things? We think it does.

For one thing, it means that there is less hurry; there is still time to take up something new and develop in a different way. This is a self-fulfilling prophecy, because we all know that the more you have to live for, the longer you are likely to live.

However good we are at maintaining strength and flexibility, there is no doubt that we are bound to deteriorate eventually, to a point where running becomes difficult and even dangerous. However, until that point is reached, it is

You are never too old to compete

our duty to ourselves, our families and our society to stay in the best possible shape for as long as possible. So go on running while you can, and when you can't run, walk, and make use of the benefits which geriatric research can offer.

The technology of hip and knee replacement gets better year by year, as does the treatment of arthritis, the treatment of eye problems and the understanding of hormone replacement treatment.

If you know that you are going to go on living into your late eighties or nineties, it is sensible to accept hip or knee replacements in your seventies, thus prolonging active life. There are already people competing seriously who have come through such replacement operations and there are likely to be a lot more of them. Bruce Davidson's story should serve as an example to us all.

Born in 1921, he was a natural athlete, excelling as a schoolboy at everything from the long jump to cross-country running. At Cambridge in 1940 he made the Varsity team in the long jump and the 880yds, but then developed pleurisy, which put an end to his running until he took it up again in his mid-sixties.

His natural ability re-asserted itself. On less than twenty miles a

101-year-old Australian Les Amey set a world age best for the 1500m at the World Veterans Championships in Brisbane in July 2001. His time was 19 mins 59 secs.

week of running, plus 50 miles a week of walking, he improved rapidly, and when he turned 70 he was in international class, winning medals in the European Veterans championships and running 43 minutes for 10k and 73 minutes for ten miles. After several years of successful running he had two artificial hip replacements, in 1999 and 2000, and now, a year after the second operation, he is embarking on his third career as a runner. Just before going to press he turned 80, and was running three times a week, about 15 miles, walking 20 miles a week, and winning his first M80 title in the British Veterans 5k championship.

If he can do it, so can you.

Twelve rules for a lifetime of running

1. Don't give up.
2. Run regularly, even if the run is short.
3. Have at least one 'quality' or speed session a week.
4. Have at least one 'endurance' run per week.
5. Use hills to maintain your leg strength.
6. Maintain flexibility and all-round strength.
7. Set plans for a year ahead.
8. Set yourself achievable targets in each phase of the year.
9. Stay off the road as much as possible.
10. Run with other people when you can.
11. If in doubt, ease off.
12. Look for new challenges every year.

APPENDIX 1

Stretching and mobility exercises

These should always be done when the muscles are warm, either after a warm-up jog or at the end of a training session. The stretching should be gradual and the stretch should be held for at least ten seconds. We have selected eight, which should be done at least three times a week.

Upper body mobility

Stand with feet apart at shoulder width and swing your arms in big circles, 10 times forwards, 10 times backwards.

Trunk mobility

With hands on hips, feet apart and knees locked, lean forwards and rotate your trunk in a wide circle, 10 times in each direction.

Calf stretch *(right)*

Stand with your hands flat up against a wall. Put one foot behind you, bending the other leg so that your upper body remains straight. Put your weight on the heel of the back foot, pushing it down to the floor

Achilles tendon stretch

Standing on one leg, with one hand on the wall, lower your body and push the knee forwards. You will feel a stretch on the lower calf and Achilles tendon.

Standing quadriceps stretch *(left)*

Standing on the left leg, grasp your right ankle with your right hand and pull it back underneath you. You should feel the stretch on the front of the quad muscle. You may use your left arm to keep yourself balanced and upright.

Hamstring stretch *(right)*

Lying on your back, raise one leg in the air and then pull the knee down towards the chest, keeping your shoulders flat on the ground.

Iliotibial band stretch *(left)*

Place one foot around the other, with both feet flat on the ground. Keeping both legs straight, lean your hips towards the side of the rearmost foot (if your right foot is at the back, lean your hips to the right). You should feel the stretch on the outside of your right leg and around the right hip.

Groin stretch *(right)*

Sit in the postion shown. Try to sit upright, pulling your heels in towards you and pressing your knees down towards the floor.

APPENDIX 2

Strength exercises

These should only be done when the muscles are thoroughly warm. They may be done with fixed weights on machines, or better still, with free weights, in which case you should be shown how to lift correctly. We recommend that you start with weights that can be lifted ten times easily.

Work progressively, increasing the weight gradually month by month until you reach a comfortable limit. Start with one set of ten of each exercise in your strength session, then move to two sets of eight, then three sets of eight. When you can manage this comfortably, move to two sets of six with a heavier weight and increase the volume gradually.

Half squat or leg extension

Standing up, feet apart, hold the weight at shoulder level. Go up onto your toes, keeping your back straight amd lower your body until your thighs are parallel with the ground, then return to start position.

Bench press

Lie on your back on a bench, with the weight held just above your chest. Straighten your arms until the elbows are locked, then return to the start.

Quadriceps curl

Sit on the end of the bench, with the knees bent and the weight across the front of your ankle. Lift the weight by straightening both legs.

Hamstring curl

Lie on your front with the weight across the back of your ankle. Pull your heels upwards until your shins are vertical, then lower again.

Sit-ups

Lie flat on the floor, or on a bench with your feet higher than your head. With arms either by your side or behind your head (more difficult), raise your trunk to a sitting position.

Power clean *(left)*

Start in the position shown. Straighten your legs first and when they are nearly straight, pull your hands up and back, so that the weight comes up to your shoulders. Return the bar to waist level, then, keeping your back straight, bend your legs until the weights touch the floor.

APPENDIX 3

Records

Britsh and World middle and long distance records

800m Men

Age	British Record		World Record		
40	P Browne	1:51.25	C Rothery	1:50.69	IRL
45	L Duffy	1:57.2	R Mercelina	1:56.16	NED
50	S Erlam	2:01.0	N Shaheed	1:58.65	USA
55	R Phipps	2:04.9	T Roberts	2:05.07	AUS
60	H Tempan	2:15.2	A Bradford	2:10.42	AUS
65	H Tempan	2:21.0	E Fee	2:14.33	CAN
70	J Todd	2:34.35	E Fee	2:20.52	CAN
75	J Todd	2:45.82	H Chapson	2:40.0	USA
80	G Porteous	3:26.1	H Chapson	2:53.5	USA
85	D Morrison	4:19.81	L Perez	3:29.42	MEX
90	J Farrell	4:38.99	A Pittendrich	4:28.20	AUS

800m Women

Age	British Record		World Record		
40	P Gallagher	2:13.02	Y Podkopayeva	1:59.25	RUS
45	P Blurton	2:14.92	Y Podkopayeva	2:02.82	RUS
50	C Oxton	2:21.9	B Lehmann	2:21.05	GER
55	C Oxton	2:22.47	C Oxton	2:22.47	GBR
60	K Stewart	2:54.2	G Van Kooten	2:36.94	NED
65	T Borthwick	2:54.5	J Horne	2:51.41	CAN
70	J Waller	3:36.41	N Naumenko	3:31.72	RUS
75	J Waller	3:43.11	N Naumenko	3:31.37	RUS
80			J Luther	3:54.81	GER
85			R Iglesias	5:00.58	MEX

1500m Men

Age	British Record		World Record		
40	R Bell	3:53.8	S Scott	3:47.64	USA
45	P Molloy	3:58.3	P Molloy	3:58.3	GBR
50	S Erlam	4:09.0	T Roberts	4:05.2	AUS
55	H Tempan	4:23.3	R Robertson	4:12.5	NZL
60	H Tempan	4:36.04	D Turnbull	4:28.66	NZL
65	H Tempan	4:44.0	S Herlaar	4:39.87	NED
70	J Todd	5:12.51	S Herlaar	4:57.65	NED
75	J Todd	5:45.43	Y Miyauchi	5:22.7	JPN
80	G Porteous	6:39.4	E Benham	6:04.28	USA
85	G Porteous	7:41.45	L Perez	7:03.38	MEX
90	J Farrell	9:23.24	J Farrell	9:23.24	USA

1500m Women

Age	British Record		World Record		
40	J Smith	4:20.7	Y Podkopayeva	3:59.78	RUS
45	P Gallagher	4:40.97	Y Podkopayeva	4:05.44	RUS
50	C Oxton	4:48.78	J Pedersen	4:43.10	SWE
55	C Oxton	4:57.4	C Oxton	4:57.4	GBR
60	J Ross	5:51.16	G Van Kooten	5:24.7	NED
65	J Ross	6:07.13	M Czerwenka-Nagel	5:57.74	GER
70	J Waller	6:47.68	N Naumenko	6:14.52	RUS
75	J Waller	7:29.3	N Naumenko	6:42.13	RUS
80			J Luther	7:32.22	GER

5000m Men

Age	British Record		World Record		
40	M McLeod	14:15.9	M Ezzher	13:43.15	FRA
45	N Gates	14:42.67	L Rault	14:23.6	FRA
50	A Amraoui	15:20.9	A Villanueva	14:55.6	MEX
55	S James	15:44.1	R Robertson	15:41.72	NZL
60	S James	16:24.0	S James	16:24.0	GBR
65	W Marshall	18:02.12	D Turnbull	16:38.8	NZL
70	W Marshall	19:16.8	D Turnbull	18:34.6	NZL
75	J Todd	20:00.13	J Todd	20:00.13	GBR
80	G Porteous	23:39.1	E Benham	21:57.88	USA
85	G Porteous	24:51.7	G Porteous	24:51.7	GBR
90	J Farrell	36:13.91	A Althaus	36:00.64	GER

5000m Women

Age	British Record		World Record		
40	P Welch	16:13.8	E Fidatov	15:20.59	ROM
45	B Cardy	17:09.3	N Leveque	15:55.71	FRA
50	J Stevenson	18:05.2	J Pedersen	17:17.02	SWE
55	M Louden	19:43.07	E Pohl	18:32.5	GER
60	J Ross	21:02.3	M Irvine	19:14.8	USA
65	J Ross	21:37.8	M Czerwenka-Nagel	21:30.1	GER
70	J Waller	23:21.1	J Waller	23:21.1	GBR
80			J Luther	28:32.67	GER

10000m Men

Age	British Record		World Record		
40	N Gates	29:43.54	M Vainio	28:30.88	FIN
45	N Gates	31:05.69	A Villanueva	30:02.56	MEX
50	L Presland	31:59.6	R Robertson	31:01.9	NZL
55	L Presland	33:10.69	R Conzelman	32:38.92	GER
60	P Morris	35:14.26	L Acquarone	34:14.88	ITA
65	S Charlton	36:48.8	D Turnbull	34:42.2	NZL
70	S Charlton	39:24.09	Ed Whitlock	38:04.10	CAN
75	D Morrison	42:03.4	D Morrison	42:03.4	GBR
80	G Porteous	48:06.0	E Benham	44:29.4	USA
85	G Porteous	55:03.48	J Galia	54:23.0	GER

10000m Women

Age	British Record		World Record		
40	J Smith	34:26.4	N Leveque	32;12.07	FRA
45	B Cardy	34:37.3	E Palm	32:34.05	SWE
50	J Stevenson	36:55.29	V Ostberg	35:37.0	NOR
55	P Fletcher	42:12.8	U Odermatt	37:19.11	SUI
60	J Ross	43:01.1	E Pohl	41:38.0	GER
65	M Louden	46:19.4	L Schultz	44:20.9	GER
70	J Waller	48:10.98	J Waller	48:10.98	GBR
80			N Naumenko	58:40.03	GER

British Veteran Age Group Bests on Road

compiled by Martin Duff

10km Men

40	Mike McLeod	29:13	Heaton	9 November 1992
45	Martin Rees	30:17	Eastleigh	15 March 1998
50	Tecwyn Davies	30:35	Reading	16 October 1988
55	Les Presland	33:05	Totton	2 October 1994
60	Steve James	33:29	Eastleigh	15 March 1997
65	Bill Stoddart	36:55	Helensbrough	22 March 1997
70	Steve Charlton	37:55	Solihull	6 October 1996
75	Gordon Porteous	45:20	Brugge	24 June 1989
80	Gordon Porteous	47:13	Perth	4 September 1994
85	Gordon Porteous	54:09	Lochinch	29 May 1999

10km Women

40	Priscilla Welch	32:14	Mobile (USA)	30 March 1985
45	Priscilla Welch	34:02	Boston (USA)	8 October 1990
50	Jeanette Stevenson	36:25	Brugge	26 June 1999
55	Joyce Smith	39:25	Gridlington	31 October 1992
60	Myfanwy Louden	43:08	Toronto (CAN)	31 October 1992*
65	Myfanwy Louden	44:20	Brugge	26 June 1999
70	Josie Waller	48:25	Newton Abbott	15 August 1993
75	Josie Waller	54:22	Oxford	18 May 1997
80	Alice Billson	73:57	Crouch End	28 April 1994
85	Alice Billson	90:13	Wargrave	14 June 1998

* Lou Gilchrist and Brenda Cook have noted two faster times on non-certified courses

Half-marathon Men

40	Paul Evans	63:15	Tyneside	6 September 2001
45	Bill Venus	65:46	Tyneside	26 May 1985
50	Tecwyn Davies	67:09	Strouds	30 October 1988
55	Evan Williams	74:16	Lake Vyrnwy	22 September 1991
60	Bill Stoddart	75:53	Arbroath	28 June 1992
65	Steve Charlton	79:49	Aylesbury	5 September 1993
70	Bill McBrinn	87:36	Ayr	8 October 2000
75	Gordon Porteous	94:06	Kirkcudbright	27 May 1989
80	Gordon Porteous	1 hr 41:35	Glasgow	21 August 1994
85	John Farrell	2 hr 17:36	Glasgow	21 August 1994

Half-marathon Women

40	Lorna Irving	71:44	Ayr	6 September 1987
45	Joyce Smith	73:06	Cambridge	15 July 1984
50	Anne Roden	80:38	Fleet	19 March 2000
55	Myfanwy Louden	87:10	Bath	17 March 1991
	and Mollie Smith	87:10	Lydd	18 October 1992
60	Mary Anstey	96:22	Stroud	29 October 1989
65	Pat Trickett	98:29	Stroud	29 October 1989
70	Josie Waller	1 hr 47:38	Exmouth	28 August 1993
75	N Richards	2 hr 12:05	Camberley	27 February 2000
80	Alice Billson	2 hr 49:34	Burnham Beeches	16 August 1998

Note: some faster times have been recorded on non-certified courses

Marathon Men

40	Ron Hill	2 hr 15:46	New Orleans	18 February 1979
45	Don McGregor	2 hr 19:10	Glasgow	30 September 1984
50	Derek Lawson	2 hr 24:58	London	20 April 1986
55	Bill McBrinn	2 hr 34:24	London	20 April 1986
60	Bill McBrinn	2 hr 46:26	Lochaber	21 April 1991
65	Hugh Currie	2 hr 51:35	Inverclyde	19 August 1990
70	John Keston	3 hr 00:58	Chicago (USA)	6 October 1996
75	Gordon Porteous	3 hr 23:12	Brugge	15 June 1989
80	Gordon Porteous	3 hr 47:04	Inverclyde	10 September 1995
85	Alf Gibson	5 hr 48:09	London	18 April 1993

Marathon Women

40	Priscilla Welch	2 hr 26:51	London	10 May 1987
45	Joyce Smith	2 hr 32:48	Los Angeles (USA)	5 August 1984
50	Anne Roden	2 hr 54:21	Boston (USA)	17 April 2000
55	Lola Smal	3 hr 14:17	Stone	2 October 1990
60	Anne Chapman	3 hr 23:37	London	21 April 1996
65	Jose Waller	3 hr 35:49	London	17 April 1988
70	Pat Trickett	3 hr 48:14	Stone	3 October 1993
75	Josie Waller	4 hr 21:40	Gosport	27 May 1997
80	Jenny Wood-Allen	5 hr 47:19	London	12 April 1992
85	Jenny Wood-Allen	6 hr 59:26	London	13 April 1997

APPENDIX 4
Useful Addresses

UK Athletics
Athletics House, 10 Harborne Road, Edgbaston, Birmingham B15 3AA
Tel: 0121 456098 Website: www.ukathletics.org

Amateur Athletic Association of England
Edgbaston House, 3 Duchess Place, Hagley Road, Birmingham B16 8NM

British Olympic Association
1 Wandsworth Place, London SW 18 1EH

South of England Athletic Association
Suite 106, City of London Fruit Exchange, Brushfield Street, London E1 6EX
Tel: 0207 247 2963

North of England Athletic Association
Suite 102, Emco House, 5/7 New York Road, Leeds LS2 7PJ
Tel: 01132 461835

Midland Counties Athletic Association
As for AAA of England

Athletics Association of Wales
Hon. Sec., Catash Road, Catsash, Newport, NP 18 1WA Tel: 01633 423833

Scottish Athletic Association
Caledonia House, Redheughs Rigg, South Gyle, Edinburgh, EH12 9DQ
Tel: 0131 317 7320

Northern Ireland Athletic Association
Athletics House, Old Coach Road, Belfast, BT 5PR Tel: 02890 60207

British Veterans Athletics Federation
Hon. Sec., 156 Mitcham Road, West Croydon, CR0 3JE
Tel: 0208 683 2602 Email: Bcushen@aol.com

British Orienteering Federation
Riversdale, Dale Road North, Darley Dale, Matlock, Derbyshire DE4 2HX
Tel: 01629 734 042

British Triathlon Association
PO Box 26, Ashby-de-la-Zouch, Leics., LE65 2ZR Tel: 01530 414234

British Association of Road Races
National Secretary, 73 Lower Bristol Road, Weston-super-mare, Avon,
BS23 2TW Tel: 01934 629911

Trail Running Association
General Secretary, Battens Farm, Clayhidon, Cullompton, Devon, EX15 3QD
Tel: 01823 680556

Fell Running Association
15 New Park View, Farsley, Pudsey, Leeds, LS28 5TZ
Tel: 0113 255 6603

Association of International Marathons
as for London Marathon

London Marathon
PO Box 1234, London, SE1 8RZ Tel: 0207 620 4117
Website: www.london-marathon.co.uk

***Rundown Events* (Race Directory)**
62 Exe Vale Road, Exeter, EX2 6LF Tel: 01392 427576
e-mail: rundown@eclipse.co.uk

***Runners World* (magazine)**
7-10 Chandos Street, London, W1M OAD Tel: 0207 291 6000
e-mail: rwedit@rodale.co.uk Website: www.runnersworld.co.uk

Athletics Weekly
Descartes Publishing Ltd., 83 Park Road, Peterborough, PE1 2TN
Tel: 01733 898440 e-mail: results@athletics-weekly.co.uk

***Running Fitness* (magazine)**
Kelsey Publishing Group, Arcade Chambers, Westgate Arcade,
Peterborough, PE1 1PY Tel: 01733 353712